KOSMOS – Discover Global Affairs

MInter Group s.r.l.
Book series on Geopolitics

Scientific Director
Michele Pavan

Editorial Management
Kaitlyn Elizabeth Rabe

Graphic Design
Federico Danesi

With contributions from Mondo Internazionale APS and Special
Eurasia

ISBN: 9798870702445

KOSMOS

Discover Global Affairs

INDEX

The America

Transnational Organised Crime and the Recent Crime Surge in Latin America

João Victor Silva Rodrigues

Abstract

This article investigates the phenomenon of transnational organised crime in four Latin American countries – Haiti, Ecuador, Colombia and Brazil – and the recent rise in violent crimes in those countries. Some definitions and interpretations of organised crime are provided, together with a brief philosophical discussion on the notion of war machines and the definition of violence. Building upon these elements, the article discusses some of the recent instances of violence in the aforementioned countries. In the final section, an analysis of the expansion of criminal organisations is conducted, coupled with some possible solutions for the issue at hand, which here will be synthesised as the need for political reforms, legal reforms and security reforms.

I.   Introduction

According to the Global Initiative against Transnational Organised Crime (GI-TOC)[1], about 83% of the global population now live in countries with a high level of crime. Latin America certainly has followed the trend, with a considerable increase in the levels of criminal activity, which makes the continent one of the most representative cores of the global criminal markets. This is corroborated by the fact that recent news reports have shown cases of extreme gang-related violence in countries such as Haiti, with the international community looking for ways to aid the country that has been traversing a tumultuous political crisis for the last two years. Considering that many other countries in the American continent are facing similar struggles with violence, one may ask whether there is a common thread there; the study that follows, therefore, will be an attempt to better understand the difficulties in dealing with crime faced by countries in Latin America.

To do so, first, a discussion about transnational organised crime will be in focus. Violence is heavily linked to drug trafficking and the activities of criminal factions, with the presence of cartels and gangs that control significant portions of some of the most important cities in the Americas. This discussion will also touch upon the concept of necropolitics, proposed originally by Achille Mbembe. Then, a summary of the most recent events in selected countries will be presented, starting with Haiti, then Ecuador, Colombia and Brazil. Afterwards, an analysis of the ongoing rise in violence will follow, combining the two previous sections while trying to shed light on the problems faced in the continent and beyond. Finally, some of the solutions proposed by the literature and reports will be addressed.

II.   Transnational organised crime: Definitions and Interpretations

Organised crime may have a plethora of definitions that can be found both in legislation and literature. In fact, some may agree that these definitions can be found in at least two

---

[1] 'Global Organized Crime Index 2023 A Fractured World' (Global Initiative Against Transnational Organized Crime (GI-TOC), 2023), https://ocindex.net/report/2023/01-global-illicit-economy.html.

different forms: a legalist approach to the concept, and an academic one[2].

The United Nations Convention Against Transnational Organised Crime, also known as the Palermo Convention of 2000, for instance, defines an "organised criminal group" as a structured group that commits one or more serious crimes to obtain financial or material gains. Moreover, they may be considered transnational if the offences committed have any connections to another state, either by encompassing other countries through the involvement of other criminal groups, or by having substantial effects elsewhere[3]. These definitions allow for wider discretion for the domestic governments of the signatories due to the variety of interpretations possible. Academic approaches, on the other hand, have sought to further explain organised crime by adding a substantial component to their conceptualisation; this has been done, for example, by analysing criminal organisations as social institutions, or social practices that compete with other human activities, while other academics focus on the formation of illegal markets[4].

According to Marco Cepik and Pedro Borba[5] organised crime can be conceived as collectives that operate crimes — normally of, but not limited to, economic motivation — regularly through the development of organisational, coercive,

---

[2] Marco Cepik and Pedro Borba, 'Crime organizado, estado e segurança internacional', *Contexto Internacional* 33, no. 2 (December 2011): 375–405, https://doi.org/10.1590/S0102-85292011000200005.; Tetiana Melnychuk, 'The Concept of Organized Crime as an Institutional Cluster', in *Organized Crime as Institutional Cluster: Transition from Traditional to Informational Model in Ukraine*, ed. Tetiana Melnychuk, SpringerBriefs in Law (Cham: Springer Nature Switzerland, 2023), 21–40, https://doi.org/10.1007/978-3-031-39532-1_3.

[3] *'United Nations Convention against Transnational Organized Crime'* (2000), United Nations: Office on Drugs and Crime, accessed 29 October 2023, //www.unodc.org/unodc/en/organized-crime/intro/UNTOC.html.

[4] Mats Berdal and Mónica Serrano, eds., *Transnational Organized Crime and International Security: Business as Usual?* (Lynne Rienner Publishers, 2002), https://doi.org/10.1515/9781626370197.; Cepik & Borba, 2011; Klaus von Lampe, *Organized Crime: Analyzing Illegal Activities, Criminal Structures and Extra-Legal Governance* (Los Angeles: SAGE, 2016); Melnychuk, 2023.

[5] Cepik & Borba, 2011

technical and political capabilities (all of which may or may not encompass illicit activities) which are functional to the execution of these crimes. Following this, networks of corruption and coercion are constitutive parts, and thus not a byproduct, of the practices of these criminal organisations[6];the use of violence as a means to achieve their goals is therefore commonplace. Furthermore, these criminal organisations conduct their operations through the recruitment of persons in vulnerable situations, such as the poor, the youth, the unemployed, orphans, immigrants, prisoners, and indigenous persons. Such conglomerates act precisely on the fragilities of the social fabric to increase their grip and influence. They are slowly stripped of their negative connotations by those who see themselves in predicaments within society, to the point that they become an alternative to the suffering, an opportunity for self-affirmation and material gain that is not afforded by living a law-abiding life. Nevertheless, criminal organisations also maintain relationships with the dominant classes and the state, which is necessary for their survival. As Cepik and Borba state, "there is as much society and state within organised crime as there is organised crime within society and the state"[7].

The relationship between organised crime and the state (or states) is almost always ambiguous. It is very common to see that the connections between criminals and politicians generate a series of interests that are mutually satisfied by the parties. To this extent, criminal organisations operate in a parasitical way within the sovereign state; they do not work to defeat or replace the state but develop their activities by taking advantage of breaches within the state, drawing upon some of the key technologies of the state. Even the state can vest itself as a criminal organisation if necessary. Hence, *de jure* sovereignty is not the key goal of organised criminal groups, as their operations are reliant on the existence of a permissive political establishment, which enables their activities to reach higher and further. Nevertheless, *de facto* sovereignty is not only attainable but it is very much in their grips in many states with weak institutions and no means to combat organised crime effectively. This led some authors to coin the concept of

---

[6] Ibid., p. 378.
[7] Ibid., p. 385

state organised crime, as was described by Henri Decœr in his book *Confronting the Shadow State*[8]. He defines it as

the use, by a public official in a position to shape or influence the actions of a state and acting in concert with a structured group, of the resources of the state to commit or facilitate the commission of acts criminalised in international law, to obtain a financial or other material benefits[9].

Thus, Decœr claims that through the convergence of interests, a mutually beneficial relationship is formed in such a way that, on the one hand, corrupt officials may benefit from financial or political support, which is especially relevant considering how these groups control significant portions of some of the largest cities in Latin America. On the other hand, those ties with government officials generate the very gaps in law enforcement where organised crime can prosper. This does not mean, however, that this relationship is carried out in the open; it is very rare to find some sort of overt collusion among the parties. In effect, the medium where this connection occurs is of extreme importance for the success of their operations. As Decœr states, the symbiosis "is often rooted in established informal practices of the high-level sphere of international business and politics that remain mostly unknown to the general public until they hit the headlines of the press"[10]. Thus, there is a grey zone between licit and illicit practices that is conducive to the existence of state organised crime and kleptocracies. Notwithstanding, outlaw groups may attack and even kill government representatives to reach their goals or eliminate potential threats to their survival, as has happened on countless occasions.

a. Necropolitics

How this symbiotic relationship functions closely resembles Achille Mbembe's description of war machines in his study of *necropolitics*, where he takes the study of biopolitics, as conceived by philosophers such as Michel Foucault[11] and

---

[8] Henri Decœur, 'The Phenomenon of State Organized Crime', in *Confronting the Shadow State: An International Law Perspective on State Organized Crime*, ed. Henri Decœur (Oxford University Press, 2018), https://doi.org/10.1093/oso/9780198823933.003.0002.

[9] Decœr, 2018, p. 15

[10] Ibid., p.18

Giorgio Agamben[12], as his starting point[13]. For Foucault, biopolitics refers to the different techniques developed by governments in order to control the population. As such, he believes that the emergence of biopolitics would mark a shift in the concept of power that is upheld by states. While the sovereign power held its highest function under the right to kill, this new phenomenon meant that the administration of the bodies of the populace became quintessential to the functioning of the state. This was the beginning of what he coined as an era of "bio-power", with "an explosion of numerous and diverse techniques for achieving the subjugation of bodies and the control of populations"[14]. This does not mean, however, that sovereign power would simply disappear, as he believes that both may coexist, but it is bio-power that gains more relevance in this historical period. Agamben departs from Foucault in that he believes that biopolitics in an integral part of sovereign power, and that is manifested by the ability of the sovereign power to reduce life to a biological minimum, something that is symbolised by the *homo sacer* (from latin "sacred man", and individual deprived of any right) in his studies[15].

Having established that, the concept of necropolitics, according to Mbembe, is an expansion on the previous notion of biopolitics. He believes that the aforementioned accounts are not enough to consider the power that the exposure to death and violence has over individuals within a state. In short, necropolitics can be defined as the practice of using death in order to subjugate individuals and populations. As evidence, he mentions the existence of "war machines", groups of armed men who may be organised or rearranged

---

[11] Michel Foucault, *The History of Sexuality*, 1st American ed (New York: Pantheon Books, 1978).

[12] Giorgio Agamben, 'Homo Sacer: Sovereign Power and Bare Life', in *Homo Sacer* (Stanford University Press, 1998), https://doi.org/10.1515/9780804764025.

[13] Achille Mbembe, 'Necropolitics', Public Culture 15, no. 1 (1 January 2003): 11–40, https://doi.org/10.1215/08992363-15-1-11.

[14] Foucault, 1978, p. 140

[15] Miguel De Larrinaga and Marc G. Doucet, 'Sovereign Power and the Biopolitics of Human Security', *Security Dialogue* 39, no. 5 (1 October 2008): 517–37, https://doi.org/10.1177/0967010608096148. The concept of *home sacer* comes from Roman law and it is used by the author to represent the life that can be killed without it constituting a crime.

according to the circumstances. They operate by seizing and controlling territories, depredating and generating currency for their affairs within and beyond the limits of their control. Furthermore, the areas controlled by those war machines operate as zones of exception within the territory of the state[16]. The relation between war machines and the state is, perhaps paradoxical, as war machines may be formed by the state, dissolved by it, supported by it or even the state may choose to transform itself into one[17]. While Mbembe's study is focused on Africa and its colonial past, it can certainly be extended to other regions of the world that went through the process of colonisation and now are suffering at the hands of armed groups.

b. *Violence*

The use of violence is possibly self-evident, with murders, assassinations kidnappings, sexual violence and other brutalities resulting from criminal gangs' doings and perhaps wars among them. How 'violence' is defined may shed light on the extent of influence these factions have over citizens' lives. It could be argued that they also perpetrate what is commonly known as structural violence. The term coined by the sociologist Johan Galtung pertains to the type of violence that is caused by the existing social structure or the institutions in a given place[18]. As Galtung suggests himself, it is closely related to social injustice[19]. By expanding the understanding of violence, it becomes clear that organised crime is not only responsible for *personal* or *direct* violence, since the control of movement of people, utilities, as well as security and life opportunities may be considered types of *structural* violence, especially in that they hamper the flourishing of individuals and limit their *capabilities* subsequent *functionings*[20]. Hence,

---

[16] Carl Schmitt, *Political Theology: Four Chapters on the Concept of Sovereignty*, University of Chicago Press ed (Chicago: University of Chicago Press, 2005).

[17] Mbembe, 2003.

[18] Johan Galtung, 'Violence, Peace, and Peace Research', *Journal of Peace Research* 6, no. 3 (1969): 167–91.

[19] Galtung, 1969, p. 171.

[20] These two concepts stem from debate in political philosophy over the 'currency' of equality. In response to other currents of thought, authors such as Amartya Sen and Martha Nussbaum argue that capabilities, defined here briefly as the real liberty individuals possess in order to achieve things that lead to a dignifying life; focusing on what each person is able to do and to be would be the

the dominion of criminal organisations, following the concept of necropolitics, leads to a life-altering exposure to violence for those who live under their control.

Considering the existence of state-organised crime and the symbiosis of the state and those groups, it is possible to conclude that, much akin to war machines, this mutually beneficial relationship also leads to the promotion of violence and death wherever they are found, especially if when taking into account the means through which different groups take over territories and enter in conflict with both police forces and rival groups. The presence of violence may also be used to the advantage of corrupt government officials, since, at first glance, it can be used to control the movements of people from and within those areas. Furthermore, providing apparent solutions to the problem of violence may prove to be popular come election time. The unfortunate reality is that very seldom those electoral promises amount to any concrete measures to eliminate (or at least curb the expansion of) criminal organisations, which begs the question of what can be done in order to solve this sort of conundrum.

III.   Countries in Latin America

While it is true that each country that suffers from the endemic violence that plagues the region merits its own in-depth study based on the historical analysis of the events, the goal of the following section will be to find the common threads for Latin America by detailing the most recent developments in some countries. This will enable the use of the discussion held in the previous section as a possible framework for better understanding those woes and provide plausible solutions. Hence, in this section, a brief overview of Haiti, Ecuador, Colombia and Brazil[21] will be established.

---

appropriate way to solve this conundrum. Further details can be found in the following: Amartya Sen, 'Equality of What?', *The Tanner Lectures on Human Values* 1, no. Cambridge University Press (22 May 1979): 195–220; Martha C. Nussbaum, 'Creating Capabilities: The Human Development Approach', in *Creating Capabilities* (Harvard University Press, 2011), https://doi.org/10.4159/harvard.9780674061200.

[21] These countries were selected due to the most recent developments and the affinity of the author with the topics presented. The glaring omission of Mexico should be of note; even though a more comprehensive study of the country would be merited, it has been discussed at length elsewhere.To that end, the reader may refer to the

a. Haiti

In recent years, Haiti has dealt with great political instability and an insurmountable increase in lawlessness, especially after the assassination of then-president Jovenel Moïse in 2021. In an interview with *The New York Times*, Daniel Foote, former US special envoy to Haiti, stated that he "would be a fool to think that narco-trafficking and arms trafficking didn't play a role in the assassination" and that "[a]nyone who understands Haiti's politics or economics understands this"[22]. The Human Rights Watch recently published a report called *Living a Nightmare*[23], discussing the recent wave of violence that has taken over Haiti. According to the report, there are approximately 300 criminal organisations operating in Haiti, and they are believed to be responsible for more than 2,000 deaths in just the first half of 2023. The majority of the killings happened in areas under control of those groups, such as the commune of Cité Soleil and the neighbourhood of Bel-Air, both located in the metropolitan area of Port-au-Prince, but also in Cabaret and Croix-des-Bouquets, two communes that fell victim to the expansion of the criminal groups. In fact, the UN estimates that they control nearly the entire metropolitan area of Port-au-Prince, a region that is house to

following: June S. Beittel, 'Mexico: Organized Crime and Drug Trafficking Organizations', *Mexico: Organized Crime and Drug Trafficking Organizations* 1 (7 June 2022): 1–43 (an interesting overview of the criminal landscape in Mexico); Nathan P. Jones, *Mexico's Illicit Drug Networks and the State Reaction* (Washington, DC: Georgetown University Press, 2016), https://search.ebscohost.com/login.aspx?direct=true&db=nlebk&AN =1238681&site=ehost-live (contains a thought-provoking discussion about the Mexican government's response to the cartels' expansion).

[22] Maria Abi-Habib, 'Haiti's Leader Kept a List of Drug Traffickers. His Assassins Came for It.', *The New York Times*, 12 December 2021, sec. World, https://www.nytimes.com/2021/12/12/world/americas/jovenel-moise-haiti-president-drug-traffickers.html. Reportedly, while the late president had been involved in corruption himself, he wished to start an anti-corruption campaign, which would not have been popular with criminals and dishonest politicians alike.

[23] Nathalye Cotrino and Ida Sawyer, "'Living a Nightmare'", ed. Anagha Neelakantan and Nīa Knighton, *Human Rights Watch*, 14 August 2023, https://www.hrw.org/report/2023/08/14/living-nightmare/haiti-needs-urgent-rights-based-response-escalating-crisis.

approximately 2.9 million[24] people, with an estimated population density of 18,296/km².

Since 2022, the two main criminal alliances in the country, the *G-Pèp* federation and the G9 alliance, have been at war against each other over the control of the territory. As the HRW report describes it, "both criminal groups that are part of these coalitions and independent groups have sought to expand their territorial control, directly attacking the population and establishing themselves as the *de facto* authorities"[25] . This resulted in increased violence for the inhabitants of the city and surrounding areas.The tactics used by the criminal organizations, however, are not limited to murder; the country has also seen an increase in sexual violence, forced displacement, looting, arson, infanticide, and kidnappings[26]. The report states that the latter in particular has turned into the main source of financing for these groups.

The lack of an adequate response by the government has led civilians to form self-defence forces, with the likes of the *Bwa Kale* being formed earlier this year. The Ministry of Justice had released a statement a month before the creation of the vigilante group reemphasising the right to legitimate self defence contained in the criminal code[27]. Alas, the operations being carried out by the group recently have devolved into more violence. The self-defence movement has been accused of carrying out killings, lynching, and indiscriminate attacks, with some victims supposedly being targeted due to their appearance or the fact that they did not live in the area they

---

[24] 'Port-Au-Prince Population 2023', accessed 2 November 2023, https://worldpopulationreview.com/world-cities/port--au--prince-population; United Nations Department of Economic and Social Affairs, 'World Urbanization Prospects The 2018 Revision', *2018*, https://population.un.org/wup/Publications/Files/WUP2018-Report.pdf.

[25] Cotrino & Sawyer, 2023, p. 17. [italics added]

[26] Jess DiPierro Obert, '"Women's Bodies Weaponized": Haiti Gangs Use Rape in Spiraling Violence', *The Guardian*, 14 November 2022, sec. World news, https://www.theguardian.com/world/2022/nov/14/haiti-gangs-violence-women-rape; Cotrino & Sawyer, 2023, p. 18-22.

[27] Ministère de la Justice et de la Securité Publique, 'MINISTÈ JISTIS AK SEKIRITE PIBLIK | NÒT POU LAPRÈS LENDI 6 MAS 2023 - Haiti MJSP', 6 March 2023, http://mjsp.gouv.ht/index.php/ministe-jistis-ak-sekirite-piblik-not-pou-lapres/.

were in[28]. Some of the crimes perpetrated by the *Bwa Kale* happened with either the help or the omission of the police forces[29]. The recent spiralling of the violence brought about by the emergence of new self-defence groups will most likely lead to the escalation of arming and recruitment, in particular of young people[30].

   b.   *Ecuador*

In October 2023, Ecuadoreans went to the polls to vote for the country's next leader. Daniel Noboa, who was announced as Guillermo Lasso's successor in the presidency of the country, is also the youngest president-elect in Ecuador's history. The elections, however, were marred by controversy as days before the first round of voting, presidential candidate Fernando Villavicencio was murdered in Quito; Villavicencio was a former journalist who made a career by speaking out against corruption. The main focus of his campaign was combating crime, corruption, and violence in the country. At the beginning of August, he revealed that he and his team had been receiving death threats, including one from the leader of *Los Choneros*, an Ecuadorian drug cartel that shares links to Colombian criminal organisations[31]. Despite the threats, he decided to move ahead with his presidential campaign. Only nine days later, he was shot dead after one of his rallies in the

---

[28] Tom Phillips and Isaac Harold, '"It's Hell": Vigilantes Take to Haiti's Streets in Bloody Reprisals against Gangs', *The Guardian*, 30 April 2023, sec. World news, https://www.theguardian.com/world/2023/apr/30/haiti-port-au-prince-violence-gangs-police; Cotrino & Sawyer, 2023, p. 22-23.

[29] Tom Phillips, 'Haiti: At Least 12 Suspected Criminals Beaten to Death and Burned in Capital', *The Guardian*, 24 April 2023, sec. World news, https://www.theguardian.com/world/2023/apr/24/haiti-at-least-12-suspected-criminals-beaten-to-death-and-burned-in-capital

[30] United Nations Integrated Office in Haiti, 'UNITED NATIONS INTEGRATED OFFICE IN HAITI: REPORT OF THE SECRETARY-GENERAL' (S/2023/492), 3 July 2023, p. 3. https://documents-dds-ny.un.org/doc/UNDOC/GEN/N23/183/33/pdf/N2318333.pdf?OpenElement

[31] AFP, 'Ecuador: Candidato presidencial Fernando Villavicencio denuncia amenazas en su contra', *El Comercio*, 1 August 2023, https://elcomercio.pe/mundo/latinoamerica/fernando-villavicencio-elecciones-ecuador-2023-candidato-presidencial-denuncia-amenazas-en-su-contra-construye-gente-buena-guillermo-lasso-los-choneros-machala-el-oro-ultimas-noticia/.

run-up to the elections. Although he was not considered to be a front-runner, his death seemed to deepen the sense of crisis started by the operations of criminal groups in the country. Six Colombian nationals were arrested in the aftermath, all of whom were believed to have ties with organised crime[32]. Mere days before citizens went to the polls, however, the suspects were killed in prison.

These events were certainly not outliers as, just weeks before the occurrence, Agustín Intriago, mayor of Manta, was assassinated in a shooting during a campaign event. A port city, Manta has been one of the cities most affected by the ongoing turf war between criminal organisations, especially owing to the fact that the control of ports is key for trafficking drugs to the United States, Europe, and other regions of the world[33]. Four suspects were arrested a month later, in addition to other arrests that had been made in the wake of the assassination; the chief of police responsible for their detentions announced that, among the detained, there were Venezuelans, Ecuadoreans, and two Dominicans. One of the implicated was a former inmate at the Guayaquil Penitentiary, with the chief stating that there had been phone calls made from the detention centre to the suspect[34].

These two murders are indicative of the surge in violence that Ecuador has experienced in recent years, where criminal factions are attempting to expand their territories and activities, all the while they enter a catastrophic war against

---

[32] Gonzalo Soriano and Regina Garcia-Cano, 'Six Colombians Arrested as Suspects in Ecuadorian Presidential Candidate's Assassination', TIME, 10 August 2023, https://time.com/6303282/ecuador-presidential-candidate-fernando-villavicencio-assassination/.
[33] Associated Press, 'Mayor of Ecuador Port City Slain in Shooting That Kills 1 Other, Wounds 4', AP News, 23 July 2023, https://apnews.com/article/ecuador-mayor-killed-gun-attack-1db25874b6882c6c9f54c96ce9e4e452;'Manta: Quién era Agustín Intriago, el alcalde asesinado a tiros en Ecuador cuya muerte conmociona al país', BBC News Mundo, 24 July 2023, https://www.bbc.com/mundo/articles/cq52yeppvy1o.
[34] 'Capturan a presuntos implicados en asesinato de Agustín Intriago tras allanamientos en Manta, Guayaquil y Naranjal', *El Universo*, 18 August 2023, sec. Noticias, https://www.eluniverso.com/noticias/ecuador/agustin-intriago-capturan-a-sospechosos-de-su-crimen-nota/.

one another. The number of killings, for instance, doubled, going from 2,495 in 2021 to 4,824 in the following year, while this figure has already reached 3,599 this year[35]. The sudden rise in violence and enlargement of the activities of drug gangs may also be driven by the increase in poverty and inequality, with one UN report affirming that "[t]he need to tackle organised crime should not obfuscate the important links between socio-economic conditions and the rise of crime" and that "[a] vicious cycle may now be emerging" as a consequence of the lack of job opportunities for the youth, working for a drug cartel becomes an appealing alternative. This, in turn, only escalates poverty, which leads to more criminality [36].

c. *Colombia*

By taking into account the fact that the majority of organised crime in Latin America cannot be constricted to the borders of states, it should come as no surprise that Ecuador, a country located between two of the world's biggest cocaine producers, namely Colombia and Peru, is dealing with the expansion of cartels. The existence of drug cartels and armed groups in Colombia is well documented. Nonethelessin 2023, the Colombian government reached an agreement on a 6-month ceasefire with the National Liberation Army (ELN). The truce is set to last until the end of January 2024, but ELN leader Aureliano Carbonell declared that the group's financing activities (which allegedly include kidnapping, drug trafficking, illegal mining and extortion) will continue[37]. For example, the ELN has recently kidnapped Colombian-born

---

[35] 'Homicidios en Ecuador', *Observatorio Ecuatoriano de Crimen Organizado (OECO)*, accessed 5 November 2023, https://oeco.padf.org/visualizador-de-datos-numero-de-homicidios/.

[36] Oliver De Schutter, 'End of Mission Statement by Mr. Olivier De Schutter Special Rapporteur on Extreme Poverty and Human Rights' (United Nations Human Rights Council, 8 September 2023), https://www.ohchr.org/sites/default/files/documents/issues/poverty/sr /statements/20230908-eom-ecuadore-sr-poverty.pdf; Dan Collyns, '"We Should Treat It as a War": Ecuador's Descent into Drug Gang Violence', *The Guardian*, 12 September 2023, sec. World news, https://www.theguardian.com/world/2023/sep/12/ecuador-violence-bloody-drug-war.

[37] Luis Jaime Acosta, 'Colombia, ELN Rebels Start Six-Month Ceasefire', *Reuters*, 3 August 2023, sec. Americas, https://www.reuters.com/world/americas/colombia-eln-rebels-start-six-month-ceasefire-2023-08-03/.

Liverpool Football Club player Luis Díaz's parents, with one of the Liberation Army leaders later admitting that the kidnapping was a mistake on their behalf. At the time of writing, his mother has been found, but his father is still missing[38].

The influence of organised crime, however, is not limited to the urban areas. For these organisations, the control of the borders is essential to facilitating trafficking and other lucrative activities. Coincidentally, many of those areas are also part of the Amazon rainforest, home to a huge diversity of fauna and flora within its biome, but also one of the most recent targets of transnational crime factions. As a result, their activities may be one of the main drivers behind the late increase of deforestation in the Amazon, as traffickers look to diversify their portfolios and control the routes used to transport illicit substances[39]. Some indigenous communities that live in the region are also feeling the effects of the expansion of criminal organisations. Reports coming from Colombia's Truth Commission suggest that indigenous peoples in Colombia have been disproportionately affected due to the long-lasting conflict between the government and the Revolutionary Armed Forces of Colombia (FARC). Since the 1970s, armed conflict in the country led paramilitary groups such as the latter to control indigenous territories with total disregard for their traditional authorities. The forced displacement, confinement, assassination of leaders, recruitment of the indigenous youth, and sexual violence followed this invasion[40]. While the Colombian government

---

[38] 'ELN reconoce "error" por secuestro del padre de Luis Díaz – DW – 04/11/2023', dw.com, accessed 5 November 2023, https://www.dw.com/es/jefe-del-eln-reconoce-error-por-secuestro-del-padre-de-luis-d%C3%ADaz/a-67305487; 'Footballer Díaz Begs Father's ELN Kidnappers to Free Him', *BBC News*, 5 November 2023, sec. Latin America & Caribbean, https://www.bbc.com/news/world-latin-america-67327414. His father was later released as previous reports suggested: Malu Cursino, 'Luis Díaz's Father Speaks for First Time since Kidnap', *BBC News*, 11 November 2023, sec. Latin America & Caribbean, https://www.bbc.com/news/world-latin-america-67390367.
[39] Robert Muggah, 'How Drugs Are Destroying the Amazon', *Foreign Policy* (blog), 6 August 2023, https://foreignpolicy.com/2023/08/06/amazon-drugs-coca-cocaine-deforestation-environment-biodiversity-climate-change-criminal-brazil-peru-colombia-bolivia-lula-logging/.

and the Farc reached a peace agreement in 2016, some members of the latter decided to continue the fight and became dissidents, creating new drug trafficking cells. This means that the violence from criminal groups against indigenous peoples in Colombia has not ceased, with the dissidents keen on recruiting young indigenous men for their knowledge of the jungle and their physical strength, something that has been disrupting the leadership organisation within the communities[41].

d. *Brazil*

The Farc dissidents are also said to have ties with Brazilian criminal organisations such as *Comando Vermelho* (CV) and *Primeiro Comando da Capital* (PCC)[42]. They operate in a similar manner to the Colombian criminals, enlisting the indigenous youth to work for them by trafficking drugs or even conducting illegal mining. Both groups are based in the southeast of Brazil (in Rio de Janeiro and São Paulo, respectively), but are responsible for operations that extend to the western borders of the country. The Brazilian government has therefore pledged 2 million soldiers to reinforce security in order to combat organised crime in the states of Mato Grosso do Sul, Mato Grosso, and Paraná[43], but in reality, it may not be enough for the fifth largest country in the world by area.

In the country's major cities, the situation is similar; in recent years, Rio de Janeiro has struggled to combat organised crime properly. The city is home to some of the largest *favelas* in the country, many of which are subjected to the control of gangs

---

[40] 'El aporte de los pueblos indígenas en la construcción de país', accessed 5 November 2023, https://web.comisiondelaverdad.co/actualidad/noticias/aporte-pueblos-indigenas-en-la-construccion-de-pais.

[41] Dimitri Selibas, 'Criminals without Borders: The Transnational Gangs Terrorising the Amazon', *The Guardian*, 9 October 2023, sec. Global development, https://www.theguardian.com/global-development/2023/oct/09/criminals-without-borders-the-transnational-gangs-terrorising-the-amazon.

[42] Ibid.

[43] 'Com 2 milhões de pessoas na região de fronteira, Exército vai reforçar segurança para combater crime organizado', G1, 1 November 2023, https://g1.globo.com/ms/mato-grosso-do-sul/noticia/2023/11/01/exercito-vai-reforcar-seguranca-na-fronteira-para-combater-crime-organizado.ghtml.

like the aforementioned CV, *Amigos dos Amigos* (ADA) and militias[44] composed of former police officers such as *Liga da Justiça* (Justice League, in English). This often results in gruesome conflicts for territory involving these factions and also the police forces[45]. As a consequence, shootouts in even some of the busiest areas of the municipality are a common occurrence. On October 23 of this year, the death of Zinho's (leader of one of the largest militia factions in Rio de Janeiro and one of the city's most wanted people) cousin during one of the Civilian Police's (*Polícia Civil* in Portuguese, or PC) operations led to serious repercussions throughout the city, with 35 buses and one train being set on fire as an act of protest by criminals. The latest incursions of police forces, due to the lack of investment, planning and solid goals that pervade them, have been called nothing more than a spectacle by some specialists, with little to no effect on the structure of the criminal organisations and their activities. The lack of funding also means that many in the police forces feel enticed to participate in operations of organised crime, either directly or indirectly[46].

São Paulo, Brazil's largest city both in terms of inhabitants and economic relevance, is also the birthplace of the most influential criminal faction in the region. The PCC was founded in 1993 by 8 inmates in one of the safest correctional facilities in the state of São Paulo[47]. They started their organisation as a reaction to the infamous Carandiru Massacre

---

[44]Ignacio Cano, 'Violence and Organized Crime in Brazil: The Case of "Militias" in Rio de Janeiro', in *Transnational Organized Crime*, ed. Heinrich Böll-Stiftung, Regine Schönenberg, and Annette von Schönfeld (Verlag, 2014), 179–88, https://doi.org/10.1515/transcript.9783839424957.179.

[45] Daiene dos Santos and Henrique Coelho, 'Operação das forças de segurança na Maré, no Alemão e na Penha tem 1 militar e 5 suspeitos mortos', G1, 20 August 2018, https://g1.globo.com/rj/rio-de-janeiro/noticia/2018/08/20/operacao-das-forcas-de-seguranca-deixa-mortos-no-rio.ghtml.

[46] Wilson Tosta, '"Narcomilícias": 8 perguntas para entender agravamento da crise de segurança no Rio', BBC News Brasil, 31 October 2023, https://www.bbc.com/portuguese/articles/cyx1zryl9vlo.

[47] Leonardo Coutinho, 'As Várias Faces Do PCC: A Origem e Evolução Da Maior Organização Criminosa Do Brasil', *Estado Da Arte* (blog), 3 May 2019, https://estadodaarte.estadao.com.br/as-varias-faces-do-pcc-a-origem-e-evolucao-da-maior-organizacao-criminosa-do-brasil/ (in Portuguese);

that had happened a year prior, in which a riot in Carandiru, the House of Detention of São Paulo, was suppressed by police battalions, resulting in the death of 111 prisoners[48]. Since then, the PCC has expanded their activities in such a way that it is no longer contained by the borders of the country. Besides the aforementioned influence in Colombia, the control of the criminal organisation encompasses other neighbouring states, with the likes of Paraguay, a strategic country for the faction, dealing with a late surge in criminality, arguably due to PCC's presence[49]. More surprising, perhaps, are the partnerships outside of Latin America that PCC has struck since its inception. A Brazilian Federal Police investigation suggests that the group has had ties with the militant group Hezbollah since as early as the year 2000[50]. Moreover, a document published by the Portuguese National Security Agency (*Serviço de Informações de Segurança* in Portuguese) reported the presence of around 1,000 people linked to PCC who live and conduct business in Portugal, which gives credence to the fact that the country is one of the most important stops in the drug trafficking route outside of the American continent. By connecting the Americas to Portugal, traffickers gain access to the European market, supplying millions of euros of illicit substances every year[51].

---

[48] 'Brazil Jail Massacre: Vigil Marks Carandiru Anniversary', *BBC News*, 2 October 2012, sec. Latin America & Caribbean, https://www.bbc.com/news/world-latin-america-19806711.

[49] Paraguay is 4th in the Global Organized Crime Index of 2023, eleven positions higher than in the previous report from 2021. Many speculate this is due to the presence of the PCC in the country. See more: 'Global Organized Crime Index 2023 A Fractured World', 2023, https://ocindex.net/report/2023/04-continental-overview.html; Cristina J. Orgaz, 'Como PCC fez Paraguai virar um dos países com maior presença de crime organizado no mundo', BBC News Brasil, 4 November 2023, https://www.bbc.com/portuguese/articles/cp646zz6z46o;

[50] Heitor Mazzoco, 'Polícia Federal investiga relações entre terroristas do Hezbollah e PCC desde os anos 2000', *O Estado de São Paulo*, 8 November 2023, sec. Blog do Fausto Macedo, https://www.estadao.com.br/politica/blog-do-fausto-macedo/policia-federal-investiga-relacoes-entre-terroristas-do-hezbollah-e-pcc-desde-os-anos-2000/ (in Portuguese); T. B. R. Newsroom, 'Brazilian Feds Crack down on Terrorist Groups Linked to Hezbollah', The Brazilian Report, 8 November 2023, https://brazilian.report/liveblog/politics-insider/2023/11/08/federal-police-terrorist-group-hezbollah/ (in English).

Nonetheless, it has been shown that the group's influence may not be limited to Portugal; in May 2023 a major crackdown by European police authorities targeting the Italian *'Ndrangheta* mafia arrested more than 100 suspects with links to criminal organisations in Latin America. More notably, clans from the *'Ndrangheta* are reportedly supplying PCC with weapons in exchange for narcotics shipments[52].

IV.   Analysis of the ongoing rise in violence and expansion of criminal organisations in Latin America

In the next section, the attention will be drawn to the main aspects of the events that were described, to discuss some of the possible solutions to the vicissitudes faced by countries in the region, and why many of the solutions that have already been suggested ultimately failed to make a significant impact.

There are some common traits among the contexts described in the previous sections, which, in fact, are recurrent themes in several countries in Latin America. The use of violence, as has been shown, is not an end for the criminal organisations, but rather a means. In some cases – as it was for Haiti and Ecuador with the deaths of Moïse, Villavicencio and Intriago – it might have been used in order to affect the political establishment. One may even ask whether or not these armed groups' end goal is to take over the government altogether; one possible response, as explained previously, is that they do not seek to have *de jure* sovereignty, meaning that they do not

---

[51] Henrique Machado, 'Crime organizado: relatório da secreta aponta para 1000 elementos do PCC a atuar em Portugal', CNN Portugal, 6 November 2023, https://cnnportugal.iol.pt/relatorio/secreta/crime-organizado-relatorio-da-secreta-aponta-para-1000-elementos-do-pcc-a-atuarem-em-portugal/20231106/65490038d34e65afa2f73fe1.

[52] Matheus Moreira, 'Mais de 100 Membros Da Máfia 'Ndrangheta Presos Na Europa', *Deutsche Welle*, 3 May 2023, sec. Europa, https://www.dw.com/pt-br/mais-de-100-membros-da-m%C3%A1fia-ndrangheta-s%C3%A3o-presos-na-europa/a-65502041 (in Portuguese); '132 'Ndrangheta Mafia Members Arrested after Investigation by Belgium Italy and Germany', Europol, accessed 9 November 2023, https://www.europol.europa.eu/media-press/newsroom/news/132-ndrangheta-mafia-members-arrested-after-investigation-belgium-italy-and-germany (in English); 'European Police Arrest More than 100 Mafia Suspects in Drug Crackdown', *Reuters*, 3 May 2023, sec. Europe, https://www.reuters.com/world/europe/dozens-arrested-germany-european-probe-italian-organised-crime-2023-05-03/ (in English).

strive to achieve any sort of legal recognition as having total control over the territory of the country and its borders. Instead, criminal organisations maintain this control in practice, within the state, and with the connivance of state officials. One could ask whether government officials stand to gain anything from their collaboration; firstly, considering the material gain that politicians may benefit from, as money laundering and even partaking in drug trafficking is not beyond them[53]. Secondly, this relationship may prove to be beneficial politically as well, as distancing or assassinating political adversaries allows dishonest officials to continue their practices and maintain the accordingly conducive *status quo* or, on a personal level, help their political ascension. As previously suggested, the state (and by extension state officials) can use war machines as a way to control politics and society, and they do so by perpetrating violence towards those who do not conform to the illicit standards that are created by the symbiotic relationship between organised crime and officials.

This can also be seen with the participation of security forces in corruption, which is not just regular, but essential for the success of the gangs' operations. In Brazil, for example, many corrupt police officers are either part of one of the militias or complicit in their activities. Others, perhaps, may choose to act in conjunction with other groups such as CV, ADA and PCC. Considering how police forces are often overworked and underpaid in Brazil and many other countries in the American continent, it is no surprise that some choose to join the criminals they were supposed to combat, considering that the latter may offer them wealth that would otherwise be unattainable by following the legal path. The riches offered by the unlawful lifestyle are also particularly alluring for the youth. Since these gangs spread especially where the presence of institutions is weak, it is often the case that they hold control over worse-off regions of the country. Thus, the opportunity of having a way out of critical life conditions is

---

[53] Tara John, 'How Corruption and Gang Warfare Transformed Ecuador', CNN, 11 August 2023, https://www.cnn.com/2023/08/11/americas/ecuador-assassination-criminal-groups-explainer-intl-latam/index.html.; 'US Bars Former Haitian Prime Minister from Entering the Country', Al Jazeera, accessed 13 November 2023, https://www.aljazeera.com/news/2023/6/2/us-bars-former-haitian-prime-minister-from-entering-the-country.

often too attractive to simply ignore. Additionally, as shown in Haiti, Ecuador, Colombia, and Brazil, some youngsters may not have a choice when faced with the overwhelming presence of organised crime where they live, something that is also true for the indigenous communities in the Amazon Rainforest.

Besides the extremely lucrative operation of drug trafficking, the activities of these illegal organisations are diverse. Kidnappings and killings are well-known; more surprisingly, however, is the fact that some groups are diversifying their crimes with deforestation and illegal mining in the Amazon. They are, unfortunately as it may be from an environmental standpoint, only joining farmers who are already involved in illicit logging and the creation of pastures in the rainforest. Despite this, there are signs that deforestation is decreasing in the Brazilian Amazon, with the government pledging to end deforestation by 2030[54]. Another important lesson to take away from the cases is how pervasive organised crime can be. Since they act where the state is mostly absent, that also means that many of the functions that the government was supposed to provide are also controlled by paramilitary groups and criminal organisations. Some groups, such as the Bwa Kale, take upon themselves the responsibility to protect citizens in the absence, or lack of ability, of the government, all the while they commit illegal acts themselves to reach this goal. In Brazilian *favelas*, moreover, many criminal groups control the supply of electricity, water, gas, transportation and even access to cable television and the internet. Since the favelas are often riddled with violence and the control of drug traffickers, many companies choose not to offer their services to those areas, leaving this burden to the criminals to provide, but also profit from it. These illegal economies mean that factions get to dictate the price of utilities, which is susceptible to unforeseen variations due to the illegal nature of the operation and the fact that factions are often in conflict with one another. One inhabitant of a shanty town was quoted as saying that he has paid traffickers for his internet connection for 10 years, citing the lack of public inspections as the main reason for that[55].

---

[54] Manuela Andreoni, 'Deforestation in the Brazilian Amazon Falls to a Five-Year Low', *The New York Times*, 10 November 2023, sec. Climate, https://www.nytimes.com/2023/11/09/climate/amazon-deforestation.html.

[55] Wilson Tosta, 'Como milícia e tráfico controlam venda de botijão em comunidades do RJ', BBC News Brasil, 26 October 2023, https://www.bbc.com/portuguese/articles/c8vl2vm6zm1o.

Furthermore, the connection between unlawful groups with their counterparts in other countries, there seems to be a consolidated network of narco-traffickers and cartels in Latin America, which is evidenced by the aforementioned influence of Brazilian and Colombian groups in Ecuador, as well as their ties and joint ventures. A 2021 report by the Global Initiative Against Transnational Organized Crime (GI-TOC) found that Mexican cartels are one of the main clients of Colombian cocaine, with the drugs acquired by them later being sold in the US market[56]. It was also demonstrated that their reach goes beyond the continent. Europe is considered to be one of the main destinations for the drugs produced across the Atlantic, and the logistics of trafficking narcotics to the old continent is at least as complex as any other process of exportation. In effect, the presence of members of Latin American factions in Europe is most likely due to the need to oversee all stages of the supply chain[57].

   a.   *What can be done about it?*
Short-term solutions to organised crime are necessary to respond to current emergencies. Mobilising police officers and the military, for instance, is one common solution, with countries such as Brazil investing in more extensive border control[58]. The conflicts between police forces and criminals are also another example, one that is very common and perhaps necessary. In spite of this, these short-term measures are unable to contain, let alone stop, the rise of gang violence. This may lead one to believe that this can only be attained

---

[56] Jeremy McDermott and James Bargent, 'The Cocaine Pipeline' (Global Initiative Against Transnational Organized Crime, February 2021).

[57] Francesco Guarascio, 'Europe Turns into Cocaine Hub as Multi-Billion-Euro Market Expands, EU Says', *Reuters*, 6 May 2022, sec. Europe, https://www.reuters.com/world/europe/europe-turns-into-cocaine-hub-multi-billion-euro-market-expands-eu-says-2022-05-06/. Other than cannabis, cocaine is the most sought after drug in Europe. It is speculated that the cocaine market in Europe is worth over 10 billion euros a year, with a significant portion of it being from South America. The same GI-TOC report also suggests that criminals have invested more in the European market due to the relative lenience when it comes to seizing narcotics and incarcerating transgressors, at least when compared to the investment made by the United States in order to curb these exports.

[58] G1, 2023

with medium and long term answers. The reports and sources used throughout this article point to two main spheres in which these types of solutions can be found: the state level and the regional/international level.

Regarding solutions at the state level[59], in order to achieve governability in Latin America, a true overhaul of institutions is necessary; the economic crises that the region faced led to the deterioration of the public sector and a subsequent decline in health, education and sanitation. The inability of the state to carry out its social functions leads the population to question the legitimacy of governments and democracy itself, and it also causes the sort of public fragility that allows criminal groups to thrive. In order to combat such dynamics, a reform is certainly due. Formulating a redistribution of political power is of paramount importance, for which three changes would be necessary: [1] "reforming the state in the strict sense by transforming its institutional structure and organisation, [2] reforming relations between the state and civil society by restructuring the means by which citizens and leaders interact, and [3] reforming political participation by transforming the mechanisms under which citizens influence state actions to guarantee real popular influence"[60]. These are without detriment to the importance of other reforms, such as that of market society, the judiciary system and citizen participation.

Applying these concepts to the countries analysed, on a domestic level, we may refer to political reforms, legal reforms, and security reforms. In terms of political reforms and in addition to the changes proposed, social assistance schemes such as universal health insurance and social welfare programs may prove to be useful in the fight against poverty and provide people with better quality of life, as well as alternatives to joining organised crime for the youth[61]. Furthermore, a more progressive taxation system, in the case of Ecuador, may be relevant considering that it could reduce the tax burden on people with low income, which, in turn, may lead to higher spending on essential goods and services,

---

[59] Carlos Blanco, 'Reform of the State: An Alternative for Change in Latin America', *The ANNALS of the American Academy of Political and Social Science* 606, no. 1 (1 July 2006): 231–43, https://doi.org/10.1177/0002716206289333.
[60] Blanco, 2006, p. 239
[61] De Schutter, 2023 provides interesting solutions in that regard.

something that might aid the economy of the country in question altogether[62]. In terms of legal reforms, one may start with changes in labour law; in countries where law enforcement is flawed, the existence of exploitative work relations may reduce the standards of living: an institutional fragility that creates an environment that criminal factions may benefit from.

The strengthening of inspections and monitoring of ports, stations and roads is of great importance in terms of security. As was discussed previously, for example, there may still be room for improvement in how the European Union has handled both the seizing of narcotics and detainment of suspects[63]. Improving the traceability of commodities originating from Latin America is another common solution found in different reports, and it should come, no less, with the subsequent penalization of the entire supply chain for illegal activities[64]. Moreover, it is essential to restrain corruption. As demonstrated in previous sections, criminal factions rely on the existence of corrupt government representatives to have successful and lucrative operations. Limiting the range of action of dishonest officials may also limit that of criminals who conspire with them, and to that end anti-corruption programs and institutions are key[65]. Other solutions such as targeting the online distribution of drugs, improving the profiling of criminal groups that act in the region of relevance, monitoring drug-related violence more extensively, and strengthening the cooperation between security forces and non-state actors would also be wise[66].

In terms of the regional and international spheres, cooperation is of the utmost significance. Given the transnational nature of organised crime, no feasible solution can be achieved without combatting all stages of the supply chain. Thus, it is

---

[62] Ibid.

[63] McDermott & Bargent, 2021; 'EU Drug Market: Cocaine' (European Monitoring Centre for Drugs and Drug Addiction (EMCDDA), May 2022), https://www.emcdda.europa.eu/publications/eu-drug-markets/cocaine_en.

[64] Muggah, 2023.

[65] United Nations Integrated Office in Haiti, 2023 is one example of a report that proposes these solutions.

[66] EMCDDA, 2022; United Nations Integrated Office in Haiti, 2023; De Schutter, 2023

indispensable to increase cooperation between the relevant actors. This can be done by enlarging the network of intelligence by creating secure ways to share information about the operations of criminal organisations in the respective regions or countries.The participation of international organisations could be beneficial as well. For example, in Haiti, the UN Security Council has approved a solution that would involve deploying Kenyan police officers in the country, although the African country is waiting until its security forces have enough training and funding from such resolution[67]. Despite indications that the level of cooperation has been on the rise between state actors, there is some margin for improvement in terms of representation when it comes to the international non-governmental actors. This may provide governments with additional tools to counter organised crime at the source since many NGOs can access areas of the major cities that may be inaccessible otherwise, and with that providing aid for those who are in need and most susceptible to the control of gangs.

The proposed solutions, albeit shortly discussed, are relevant but are not the only possibilities. Regardless, they all point to a more holistic approach to the fight against organised crime and violence in Latin America. It is not feasible to reach any sort of advancement in the matter without a thorough and well-coordinated program that entails political and legal reforms, as well as enhancing security and international cooperation. Here, however, lies a problem: how is it possible to conduct such a comprehensive package of programs in countries where the institutions are unreliable? Many countries in Latin America have suffered from endemic corruption for years. It begs the question of whether or not these reforms would hold in those political establishments. Furthermore, there is a perceived lack of continuity in terms of political programmes with leadership changes. Even if a long-term programme is started to root out corruption and monitor drug trafficking more intensely, there are no guarantees that the following leader will follow up on the projects of their predecessors, especially considering that those long-term

---

[67] 'Kenya Says It Won't Deploy Police to Fight Gangs in Haiti until They Receive Training and Funding', AP News, 9 November 2023, https://apnews.com/article/kenya-haiti-armed-force-police-gangs-279576af14799ded2494e18b97a3054b.

solutions may not be as popular in the ballots as an immediate response to the issue.

While this is surely a small sample size, it should provide enough background to analyse the issues at hand. Haiti, Ecuador, Colombia and Brazil were selected due to the most recent developments and the affinity of the author with the topics presented. The omission of Mexico should be of note; even though a more comprehensive study of the country would be merited, it was not pursued here due to the brevity of this article. Nonetheless, it remains an interesting opportunity for further research[68].

---

[68] June S. Beittel, 'Mexico: Organized Crime and Drug Trafficking Organizations', *Mexico: Organized Crime and Drug Trafficking Organizations* 1 (7 June 2022): 1–43 (an interesting overview of the criminal landscape in Mexico); Nathan P. Jones, *Mexico's Illicit Drug Networks and the State Reaction* (Washington, DC: Georgetown University Press, 2016), https://search.ebscohost.com/login.aspx?direct=true&db=nlebk&AN =1238681&site=ehost-live (contains a thought-provoking discussion about the Mexican government's response to the cartels' expansion)

Bibliography

Abi-Habib, Maria. 'Haiti's Leader Kept a List of Drug Traffickers. His Assassins Came for It.' *The New York Times*, 12 December 2021, sec. World. https://www.nytimes.com/2021/12/12/world/americas/jovenel-moise-haiti-president-drug-traffickers.html.

Acosta, Luis Jaime. 'Colombia, ELN Rebels Start Six-Month Ceasefire'. *Reuters*, 3 August 2023, sec. Americas. https://www.reuters.com/world/americas/colombia-eln-rebels-start-six-month-ceasefire-2023-08-03/.

AFP. 'Ecuador: Candidato presidencial Fernando Villavicencio denuncia amenazas en su contra'. *El Comercio*, 1 August 2023. https://elcomercio.pe/mundo/latinoamerica/fernando-villavicencio-elecciones-ecuador-2023-candidato-presidencial-denuncia-amenazas-en-su-contra-construye-gente-buena-guillermo-lasso-los-choneros-machala-el-oro-ultimas-noticia/.

Agamben, Giorgio. 'Homo Sacer: Sovereign Power and Bare Life'. In *Homo Sacer*. Stanford University Press, 1998. https://doi.org/10.1515/9780804764025.

Al Jazeera. 'US Bars Former Haitian Prime Minister from Entering the Country'. Accessed 13 November 2023. https://www.aljazeera.com/news/2023/6/2/us-bars-former-haitian-prime-minister-from-entering-the-country.

Andreoni, Manuela. 'Deforestation in the Brazilian Amazon Falls to a Five-Year Low'. *The New York Times*, 10 November 2023, sec. Climate. https://www.nytimes.com/2023/11/09/climate/amazon-deforestation.html.

AP News. 'Kenya Says It Won't Deploy Police to Fight Gangs in Haiti until They Receive Training and Funding', 9 November 2023. https://apnews.com/article/kenya-haiti-armed-force-police-gangs-279576af14799ded2494e18b97a3054b.

Associated Press. 'Mayor of Ecuador Port City Slain in Shooting That Kills 1 Other, Wounds 4'. AP News, 23 July

2023. https://apnews.com/article/ecuador-mayor-killed-gun-attack-1db25874b6882c6c9f54c96ce9e4e452

BBC News. 'Brazil Jail Massacre: Vigil Marks Carandiru Anniversary'. 2 October 2012, sec. Latin America & Caribbean. https://www.bbc.com/news/world-latin-america-19806711.

BBC News. 'Footballer Díaz Begs Father's ELN Kidnappers to Free Him'. 5 November 2023, sec. Latin America & Caribbean. https://www.bbc.com/news/world-latin-america-67327414.

BBC News. 'Haiti Arrests Key Suspect in President Jovenel Moise's Murder'. 20 October 2023, sec. Latin America & Caribbean. https://www.bbc.com/news/world-latin-america-67168562.

BBC News Mundo. 'Manta: Quién era Agustín Intriago, el alcalde asesinado a tiros en Ecuador cuya muerte conmociona al país', 24 July 2023. https://www.bbc.com/mundo/articles/cq52yeppvy1o.

Beittel, June S. 'Mexico: Organized Crime and Drug Trafficking Organizations'. *Mexico: Organized Crime and Drug Trafficking Organizations* 1 (7 June 2022): 1–43.

Berdal, Mats, and Mónica Serrano, eds. *Transnational Organized Crime and International Security: Business as Usual?* Lynne Rienner Publishers, 2002. https://doi.org/10.1515/9781626370197.

Blanco, Carlos. 'Reform of the State: An Alternative for Change in Latin America'. *The ANNALS of the American Academy of Political and Social Science* 606, no. 1 (1 July 2006): 231–43. https://doi.org/10.1177/0002716206289333.

Cano, Ignacio. 'Violence and Organized Crime in Brazil: The Case of "Militias" in Rio de Janeiro'. In *Transnational Organized Crime*, edited by Heinrich Böll-Stiftung, Regine Schönenberg, and Annette von Schönfeld, 179–88. Verlag, 2014. https://doi.org/10.1515/transcript.9783839424957.179.

Cepik, Marco, and Pedro Borba. 'Crime organizado, estado e segurança internacional'. *Contexto Internacional* 33, no. 2

(December 2011): 375–405. https://doi.org/10.1590/S0102-85292011000200005.

Collyns, Dan. '"We Should Treat It as a War": Ecuador's Descent into Drug Gang Violence'. *The Guardian*, 12 September 2023, sec. World news. https://www.theguardian.com/world/2023/sep/12/ecuador-violence-bloody-drug-war.

Cotrino, Nathalye, and Ida Sawyer. '"Living a Nightmare"'. Edited by Anagha Neelakantan and Nīa Knighton. *Human Rights Watch*, 14 August 2023. https://www.hrw.org/report/2023/08/14/living-nightmare/haiti-needs-urgent-rights-based-response-escalating-crisis.

'Countries with the Highest Criminality Rate in the World - The Organized Crime Index'. Accessed 9 November 2023. https://ocindex.net/.

Coutinho, Leonardo. 'As Várias Faces Do PCC: A Origem e Evolução Da Maior Organização Criminosa Do Brasil'. *Estado Da Arte* (blog), 3 May 2019. https://estadodaarte.estadao.com.br/as-varias-faces-do-pcc-a-origem-e-evolucao-da-maior-organizacao-criminosa-do-brasil/.

Cursino, Malu. 'Luis Díaz's Father Speaks for First Time since Kidnap'. *BBC News*, 11 November 2023, sec. Latin America & Caribbean. https://www.bbc.com/news/world-latin-america-67390367.

De Larrinaga, Miguel, and Marc G. Doucet. 'Sovereign Power and the Biopolitics of Human Security'. *Security Dialogue* 39, no. 5 (1 October 2008): 517–37. https://doi.org/10.1177/0967010608096148.

De Schutter, Oliver. 'End of Mission Statement by Mr. Olivier De Schutter Special Rapporteur on Extreme Poverty and Human Rights'. United Nations Human Rights Council, 8 September 2023. https://www.ohchr.org/sites/default/files/documents/issues/poverty/sr/statements/20230908-eom-ecuadore-sr-poverty.pdf.

Decoeur, Henri. 'The Phenomenon of State Organized Crime'. In *Confronting the Shadow State: An International Law Perspective on State Organized Crime*, edited by Henri Decoeur, 0. Oxford University Press, 2018. https://doi.org/10.1093/oso/9780198823933.003.0002.

dw.com. 'ELN reconoce "error" por secuestro del padre de Luis Díaz – DW – 04/11/2023'. Accessed 5 November 2023. https://www.dw.com/es/jefe-del-eln-reconoce-error-por-secuestro-del-padre-de-luis-d%C3%ADaz/a-67305487.

'El aporte de los pueblos indígenas en la construcción de país'. Accessed 5 November 2023. https://web.comisiondelaverdad.co/actualidad/noticias/aporte-pueblos-indigenas-en-la-construccion-de-pais.

El Universo. 'Capturan a presuntos implicados en asesinato de Agustín Intriago tras allanamientos en Manta, Guayaquil y Naranjal'. 18 August 2023, sec. Noticias. https://www.eluniverso.com/noticias/ecuador/agustin-intriago-capturan-a-sospechosos-de-su-crimen-nota/.

'EU Drug Market: Cocaine'. European Monitoring Centre for Drugs and Drug Addiction, May 2022. https://www.emcdda.europa.eu/publications/eu-drug-markets/cocaine_en.

Europol. '132 'Ndrangheta Mafia Members Arrested after Investigation by Belgium Italy and Germany'. Accessed 9 November 2023. https://www.europol.europa.eu/media-press/newsroom/news/132-ndrangheta-mafia-members-arrested-after-investigation-belgium-italy-and-germany.

Foucault, Michel. *The History of Sexuality*. 1st American ed. New York: Pantheon Books, 1978.

G1. 'Com 2 milhões de pessoas na região de fronteira, Exército vai reforçar segurança para combater crime organizado', 1 November 2023. https://g1.globo.com/ms/mato-grosso-do-sul/noticia/2023/11/01/exercito-vai-reforcar-seguranca-na-fronteira-para-combater-crime-organizado.ghtml.

Galtung, Johan. 'Violence, Peace, and Peace Research'. *Journal of Peace Research* 6, no. 3 (1969): 167–91.

'Global Organized Crime Index 2023 A Fractured World'. Global Initiative Against Transnational Organized Crime (GI-TOC), 2023. https://ocindex.net/report/2023/04-continental-overview.html.

Gonzalo Soriano and Regina Garcia-Cano. 'Six Colombians Arrested as Suspects in Ecuadorian Presidential Candidate's Assassination'. TIME, 10 August 2023. https://time.com/6303282/a-presidential-candidate-in-ecuador-has-been-assassinated/.

Guarascio, Francesco. 'Europe Turns into Cocaine Hub as Multi-Billion-Euro Market Expands, EU Says'. *Reuters*, 6 May 2022, sec. Europe. https://www.reuters.com/world/europe/europe-turns-into-cocaine-hub-multi-billion-euro-market-expands-eu-says-2022-05-06/.

Hughes, Eléonore. 'Five Years after Rio Councilwoman Slain, Questions and Hope'. AP News, 14 March 2023. https://apnews.com/article/brazil-marielle-councilwoman-anniversary-five-years-lula-bolsonaro-b35bacc44318f34a9f77adce8cece652.

John, Tara. 'How Corruption and Gang Warfare Transformed Ecuador'. CNN, 11 August 2023. https://www.cnn.com/2023/08/11/americas/ecuador-assassination-criminal-groups-explainer-intl-latam/index.html.

Jones, Nathan P. *Mexico's Illicit Drug Networks and the State Reaction*. Washington, DC: Georgetown University Press, 2016. https://search.ebscohost.com/login.aspx?direct=true&db=nlebk&AN=1238681&site=ehost-live.

Lampe, Klaus von. *Organized Crime: Analyzing Illegal Activities, Criminal Structures and Extra-Legal Governance*. Los Angeles: SAGE, 2016.

Machado, Henrique. 'Crime organizado: relatório da secreta aponta para 1000 elementos do PCC a atuar em Portugal'. CNN Portugal, 6 November 2023. https://cnnportugal.iol.pt/relatorio/secreta/crime-organizado-relatorio-da-secreta-aponta-para-1000-elementos-do-pcc-a-atuarem-em-portugal/20231106/65490038d34e65afa2f73fe1.

Mazzoco, Heitor. 'Polícia Federal investiga relações entre terroristas do Hezbollah e PCC desde os anos 2000'. *O Estado de São Paulo*, 8 November 2023, sec. Blog do Fausto Macedo. https://www.estadao.com.br/politica/blog-do-fausto-macedo/policia-federal-investiga-relacoes-entre-terroristas-do-hezbollah-e-pcc-desde-os-anos-2000/.

Mbembe, Achille. 'Necropolitics'. *Public Culture* 15, no. 1 (1 January 2003): 11–40. https://doi.org/10.1215/08992363-15-1-11.

McDermott, Jeremy, and James Bargent. 'The Cocaine Pipeline'. Global Initiative Against Transnational Organized Crime, February 2021.

Melnychuk, Tetiana. 'Basic Approaches to Organized Crime Conceptualization'. In *Organized Crime as Institutional Cluster: Transition from Traditional to Informational Model in Ukraine*, edited by Tetiana Melnychuk, 11–19. SpringerBriefs in Law. Cham: Springer Nature Switzerland, 2023. https://doi.org/10.1007/978-3-031-39532-1_2.

———. 'Introduction'. In *Organized Crime as Institutional Cluster: Transition from Traditional to Informational Model in Ukraine*, edited by Tetiana Melnychuk, 1–9. SpringerBriefs in Law. Cham: Springer Nature Switzerland, 2023. https://doi.org/10.1007/978-3-031-39532-1_1.

———. 'The Concept of Organized Crime as an Institutional Cluster'. In *Organized Crime as Institutional Cluster: Transition from Traditional to Informational Model in Ukraine*, edited by Tetiana Melnychuk, 21–40. SpringerBriefs in Law. Cham: Springer Nature Switzerland, 2023. https://doi.org/10.1007/978-3-031-39532-1_3.

———. 'The Contemporary Hybrid Model and Organized Crime Clusters'. In *Organized Crime as Institutional Cluster: Transition from Traditional to Informational Model in Ukraine*, edited by Tetiana Melnychuk, 97–117. SpringerBriefs in Law. Cham: Springer Nature Switzerland, 2023. https://doi.org/10.1007/978-3-031-39532-1_5.

Ministère de la Justice et de la Securité Publique. 'MINISTÈ JISTIS AK SEKIRITE PIBLIK | NÒT POU LAPRÈS LENDI 6 MAS 2023 - Haiti MJSP', 6 March 2023. http://mjsp.gouv.ht/index.php/ministe-jistis-ak-sekirite-piblik-not-pou-lapres/.

Moreira, Matheus. 'Mais de 100 Membros Da Máfia 'Ndrangheta Presos Na Europa'. *Deutsche Welle*, 3 May 2023, sec. Europa. https://www.dw.com/pt-br/mais-de-100-membros-da-m%C3%A1fia-ndrangheta-s%C3%A3o-presos-na-europa/a-65502041.

Muggah, Robert. 'How Drugs Are Destroying the Amazon'. *Foreign Policy* (blog), 6 August 2023. https://foreignpolicy.com/2023/08/06/amazon-drugs-coca-cocaine-deforestation-environment-biodiversity-climate-change-criminal-brazil-peru-colombia-bolivia-lula-logging/.

Nussbaum, Martha C. 'Creating Capabilities: The Human Development Approach'. In *Creating Capabilities*. Harvard University Press, 2011. https://doi.org/10.4159/harvard.9780674061200.

Obert, Jess DiPierro. '"Women's Bodies Weaponized": Haiti Gangs Use Rape in Spiraling Violence'. *The Guardian*, 14 November 2022, sec. World news. https://www.theguardian.com/world/2022/nov/14/haiti-gangs-violence-women-rape.

OECO. 'Homicidios en Ecuador'. Accessed 5 November 2023. https://oeco.padf.org/visualizador-de-datos-numero-de-homicidios/.

Orgaz, Cristina J. 'Como PCC fez Paraguai virar um dos países com maior presença de crime organizado no mundo'. BBC News Brasil, 4 November 2023. https://www.bbc.com/portuguese/articles/cp646zz6z46o.

Phillips, Tom. 'Haiti: At Least 12 Suspected Criminals Beaten to Death and Burned in Capital'. *The Guardian*, 24 April 2023, sec. World news. https://www.theguardian.com/world/2023/apr/24/haiti-at-least-12-suspected-criminals-beaten-to-death-and-burned-in-capital.

Phillips, Tom, and Harold Isaac. '"It's Hell": Vigilantes Take to Haiti's Streets in Bloody Reprisals against Gangs'. *The Guardian*, 30 April 2023, sec. World news. https://www.theguardian.com/world/2023/apr/30/haiti-port-au-prince-violence-gangs-police.

'Port-Au-Prince Population 2023'. Accessed 2 November 2023. https://worldpopulationreview.com/world-cities/port--au--prince-population.

Reuters. 'Colombia Killings of Social Leaders Hit Record in 2022 -Ombudsman'. 23 January 2023, sec. Americas. https://www.reuters.com/world/americas/colombia-killings-social-leaders-hit-record-2022-ombudsman-2023-01-23/.

Reuters. 'European Police Arrest More than 100 Mafia Suspects in Drug Crackdown'. 3 May 2023, sec. Europe. https://www.reuters.com/world/europe/dozens-arrested-germany-european-probe-italian-organised-crime-2023-05-03/.

Sanchez R., Magaly. 'Insecurity and Violence as a New Power Relation in Latin America'. *Annals of the American Academy of Political and Social Science* 606 (2006): 178–95.

Santos, Daiene dos, and Henrique Coelho. 'Operação das forças de segurança na Maré, no Alemão e na Penha tem 1 militar e 5 suspeitos mortos'. G1, 20 August 2018. https://g1.globo.com/rj/rio-de-janeiro/noticia/2018/08/20/operacao-das-forcas-de-seguranca-deixa-mortos-no-rio.ghtml.

Schmitt, Carl. *Political Theology: Four Chapters on the Concept of Sovereignty*. University of Chicago Press ed. Chicago: University of Chicago Press, 2005.

Selibas, Dimitri. 'Criminals without Borders: The Transnational Gangs Terrorising the Amazon'. *The Guardian*, 9 October 2023, sec. Global development. https://www.theguardian.com/global-development/2023/oct/09/criminals-without-borders-the-transnational-gangs-terrorising-the-amazon.

Sen, Amartya. 'Equality of What?' Edited by Sterling McMurrin. *The Tanner Lectures on Human Values* 1, no. Cambridge University Press (22 May 1979): 195–220.

Statista. 'Population of Latin American Countries 2022'. Accessed 14 November 2023. https://www.statista.com/statistics/988453/number-inhabitants-latin-america-caribbean-country/.

Taylor, Luke. '"There's No Police or State": Haitians Helpless as Violence and Brutality Soars'. *The Guardian*, 14 August 2023, sec. World news. https://www.theguardian.com/world/2023/aug/14/haiti-violence-abuse-killing-human-rights-watch.

TBR Newsroom. 'Brazilian Feds Crack down on Terrorist Groups Linked to Hezbollah'. The Brazilian Report, 8 November 2023. https://brazilian.report/liveblog/politics-insider/2023/11/08/federal-police-terrorist-group-hezbollah/.

Tosta, Wilson. 'Como milícia e tráfico controlam venda de botijão em comunidades do RJ'. BBC News Brasil, 26 October 2023. https://www.bbc.com/portuguese/articles/c8vl2vm6zm1o.

———. '"Narcomilícias": 8 perguntas para entender agravamento da crise de segurança no Rio'. BBC News Brasil, 31 October 2023. https://www.bbc.com/portuguese/articles/cyx1zryl9vlo.

'Transnational Organized Crime: Analyses of a Global Challenge to Democracy'. In *Transnational Organized Crime.* transcript Verlag, 2014. https://doi.org/10.1515/transcript.9783839424957.

United Nations Department of Economic and Social Affairs. 'World Urbanization Prospects The 2018 Revision'. *2018*, n.d.

United Nations Integrated Office in Haiti. 'United Nations Integrated Office in Haiti: Report of the Secretary-General', 3 July 2023. https://documents.un.org/prod/ods.nsf/xpSearchResultsM.xsp.

United Nations Office on Drugs and Crime. 'United Nations Convention against Transnational Organized Crime'.

Accessed 29 October 2023. //www.unodc.org/unodc/en/organized-crime/intro/UNTOC.html.

Willis, Graham Denyer. *The Killing Consensus: Police, Organized Crime, and the Regulation of Life and Death in Urban Brazil.* 1st ed. University of California Press, 2015. https://www.jstor.org/stable/10.1525/j.ctt13x1hrn.
'World Urbanization Prospects - Population Division - United Nations'. Accessed 2 November 2023. https://population.un.org/wup/Publications/.

__João Victor Silva Rodrigues__ is a junior researcher for the G.E.O. division at Mondo Internazionale and a master's degree student at the University of Milan, where he was awarded the Academic Excellence Scholarship for the university's Politics, Philosophy and Public Affairs degree. Having graduated in International Relations at Ibmec, Brazil, he worked as an undergraduate teaching assistant for the International Relations Theory course. In the past, he researched about the development of Christian practices in China, Chinese history and pop culture and soft power in Japan. His current research interests are political solidarity, postcolonial studies, International Relations Theory, as well as regional studies of Latin America, Southeast Asia and Africa.

Europe

Deterrence, Defence and Arms Control: what is at stake in the current security agenda?

Giacomo Andolfatto

Abstract

The return of great power competition has brought nuclear weapons back to the global political agenda, given by the threats from the Russian Federation, aiming at deterring NATO from supporting Ukraine from one hand, and the Rise of China as a nuclear power on the other. The current security environment represents a challenge for the North Atlantic Treaty Organisation, which needs to adapt to these issues. The aim of the chapter is to better understand the role of nuclear weapons as an essential part of the Alliance's resources in ensuring a credible and efficient deterrent. It will proceed with a brief analysis on the Chinese current military buildup, and how it will have an impact on the Alliance's strategy. Finally, this study will concentrate on current arms control treaties, reviewing the current state of the art, along with a brief review on the possible developments ahead.

Keywords: Deterrence, Nuclear Weapons, Arms Control, NATO, China.

The war in Ukraine has brought the threat of using nuclear weapons to the discussions' table, marking "a true end of the post-Cold War era, a time when the nuclear arsenals of Russia and the United States were significantly downsized and the role of nuclear weapons was de-emphasised".[1] Many experts have debated on the conditions that will lead Moscow to use its nuclear arsenal, as Putin's intimidations to deter NATO from intervening or supporting Ukraine are "the most significant attempt at prolonged, consistent, and conscious nuclear coercion against NATO and its partners in almost forty years".[2]

But the Russian threat to the European security architecture is just one of the challenges posed by this new security environment. In fact, along with the increasing pressure from the Democratic Republic of Korea's missile tests; Iran's developments on its nuclear programme; and the fragile balance between Pakistan and India, the expansion of the People's Republic of China's (PRC) nuclear arsenal is another important factor to take into consideration. In recent years, Beijing has increased its capabilities, building new silos for intercontinental ballistic missiles (ICBMs), and developing new types of delivery systems.[3] Clearly, such a quantitative and qualitative expansion demands even more attention, especially from NATO countries. [4] The European security architecture has changed, requiring NATO's European countries to boost their own expenditures on defence, reaching "an all-time yearly high of $2240 billion", to address capability shortfalls.[5] Especially through the launch of several

---

[1] Gilli, Andrea, and De Dreuzy, Pierre (eds.), *Nuclear strategy in the 21st century: continuity or change?*, (NATO Defense College, Rome, 2022), xvi.

[2] Gilli, Andrea, and De Dreuzy, Pierre, "Russia's nuclear coercion in Ukraine", *NATO Review*, November 29, 2022, https://www.nato.int/docu/review/articles/2022/11/29/russias-nuclear-coercion-in-ukraine/index.html .

[3] Wright, Timothy, "Is China gliding toward a FOBS capability?", *International Institute for Security Studies (IISS)*, Online Analysis, October 22, 2021, https://www.iiss.org/online-analysis/online-analysis/2021/10/is-china-gliding-toward-a-fobs-capability/ .

[4] Bugos, Shannon, and Masterson, Julia, "New Chinese Missile Silo Fields Discovered", *Arms Control Association*, September, 2021, https://www.armscontrol.org/act/2021-09/news/new-chinese-missile-silo-fields-discovered .

[5] Naughtie, Andrew, and Baniya, Sudesh, "Europe's military spending soars, fuelled by Ukraine war", Euronews, 24 April 24,

initiatives within common fora for building and buying weapons together, for a common purpose (strengthening European assets and capabilities), European leaders are further realising the need to reinvigorate their capabilities, in order to ensure a credible deterrent to possible adversaries, without relying too much on the United States, especially if the latter will engage in other critical theatres, such as the Indo-Pacific.[67]

NATO nuclear countries had to consider a general review of their nuclear policies too, in case of an increased threat. On the one hand, France decided to ensure a more "concrete dissuasion", by adapting its arsenal to the current international security environment, such as by modernising new types of submarine-launched ballistic missiles (SLBMs), while respecting its "strict sufficiency" principle (i.e., keeping its nuclear arsenal at the lowest possible level, in accordance with the strategic context).[89] Similarly, the United Kingdom has emphasised the need to upgrade its arsenal, while ensuring that it will be used "only in extreme circumstances if self-defence, including [of our] NATO allies".[10]

2023, https://www.euronews.com/2023/04/24/europes-military-spending-soars-fuelled-by-ukraine-war .

[6] Andersson, Jan Joel, "Building Weapons Together (or not)", *EUISS*, Brief, November 16, 2023, https://www.iss.europa.eu/content/building-weapons-together-or-not . See also Andersson, Jan Joel, "Buying weapons together (or not): Joint defense acquisition and parallel arms procurement", *EUISS*, Brief, April 3, 2023, https://www.iss.europa.eu/content/buying-weapons-together-or-not .

[7] Loss, Rafael, and Mehrer, Angela, "Striking absence: Europe's missile gap and how to close it", *ECFR*, November 21, 2023, https://ecfr.eu/article/striking-absence-europes-missile-gap-and-how-to-close-it/ .

[8] Republique Française, "Revue nationale stratégique", 2022. See also Vavasseur, Xavier, "France Successfully Test-Fires New M51.3 SLBM", *Naval News*, 19 November 19, 2023, https://www.navalnews.com/naval-news/2023/11/france-successfully-test-fires-new-m51-3-slbm/ .

[9] "What France achieved", *France TNP*, https://www.francetnp.gouv.fr/what-france-achieved?lang=fr .

[10] HM Government, "Integrated Review Refresh 2023: Responding to a more contested and volatile world", March, 2023, https://assets.publishing.service.gov.uk/government/uploads/system/uploads/attachment_data/file/1145586/11857435_NS_IR_Refresh_2023_Supply_AllPages_Revision_7_WEB_PDF.pdf .

Today's international agenda is presenting a fragile multipolar nuclear world, in which NATO needs to reflect on whether its deterrence strategy will be credible in the future, and if it will be the best for addressing those challenges presented by new nuclear peers, such as China. Thus, the current chapter aims at better understanding the increasing relevance of deterrence in today's international arena. First, this analysis will start by analysing one of NATO's core pillars, that of deterrence and defence. From this initial description, it will concentrate on the increasing role of the Chinese nuclear arsenal. Finally, the last paragraph will provide a brief outlook on arms control, reflecting on some possible developments on the matter.

I.   NATO and its foundations

NATO is living in a critical moment. If from one side it has been highlighted the need for the Alliance to focus on resilience, on the other it has been emphasized the need to return to its original task of collective defence.[11] In order to better understand what the best options for the Alliance would be, it is important to briefly describe what are its founding principles.

a. The Alliance's three main pillars

Since its foundation, the Atlantic Alliance has rooted its functioning around three main principles, all based on strategic documents such as the Strategic Concept:[12]

1. Deterrence and Defence, which ensures mutual assistance among Allies against a foreign attack or a challenge that is threatening one or more member States. As confirmed by Article 5 of the Washington Treaty, the principle of collective defence has been one of the founding principles of the Atlantic Alliance, that has enhanced its collective readiness and responsiveness towards any security challenge against its own members, "based on an appropriate mix of nuclear, conventional and missile defence capabilities, complemented with space and cyber capabilities".[13]

2. Crisis Prevention and Management: this pillar aims at showing the willingness of the Alliance to address all kinds of crises that might have an impact on the Organisation's security. Following the operations in the Balkans, the Alliance conducted other operations

---

[11] Jankowsky, Dominik P. (edited by), "NATO and the future of arms control", (NATO Defense College, Rome, 2021). See also Coker, Christoher, "Why NATO should return home. The case for a twenty-first century alliance", *The RUSI Journal*, 153, No. 4, (2008), pp. 6-11.

[12] Pedlow, Gregory W., "NATO strategy documents: 1949-1969", *NATO International Staff Central Archives*, 1999. See also Ruiz-Palmer, Diego, "A strategy odyssey: constancy of purpose and strategy-making in NATO, 1949-2019", (NATO Defense College, Rome, 2019).

[13] NATO, *2022 Strategic Concept*, June 29, 2022, https://www.nato.int/nato_static_fl2014/assets/pdf/2022/6/pdf/29062 2-strategic-concept.pdf .

of crisis management in Libya and Afghanistan – although with uncertain results.[14]

3. Finally, the principle of Cooperative Security: this principle aims at strengthening NATO's relations with its partners, while ensuring its own security. This principle is then translated into stronger political and diplomatic relations, aimed at supporting NATO's crisis management and prevention activities, as well as other challenges faced by both the Alliance and its partners.

For the purpose of this analysis, we will focus only on the first founding pillar of the Atlantic Alliance, first by describing the importance of nuclear weapons as part of the mix for a credible NATO deterrent, then by providing a brief analysis on a challenge that might have an impact on the principle of Deterrence and Defence, especially considering the nuclear domain: the expansion of the Chinese nuclear arsenal.

a. A focus on the first pillar: Deterrence & Defence and nuclear weapons

Nuclear weapons play an important role in NATO's deterrence & defence and represent an essential component, to guarantee a credible deterrent. To be clear, NATO is a nuclear alliance, but it does not "own" a nuclear arsenal. Rather, the Alliance counts on three nuclear powers among its members, namely the United States, the United Kingdom, and France, and their independent nuclear deterrents contribute to the overall NATO deterrent. The Alliance's nuclear posture mainly relies on the Unites States' nuclear weapons deployed in Europe since the 1950s (more precisely, a set of B61 gravity bombs). Along with the stationing of nuclear weapons, NATO is characterised by a procedure known as "nuclear sharing", which gives the possibility for allied launchers to carry U.S. nuclear weapons (today, Dual-Capable Aircrafts – DCA).[15] This represents a unique feature, as it demonstrates cohesion among Allies within the organisation, demonstrated by the shared burden given by nuclear weapons.

---

[14] Rühle, Michael, "Crisis Management in NATO", European Security, Vol. 2, No. 4 (1993), pp. 491-501.
[15] Tertrais, Bruno, "Principles of Nuclear Deterrence and Strategy", (NATO Defense College, Rome, 2021).

To further show cooperation among Allies, since 1966 NATO provides a forum where to exchange information among allies: the Nuclear Planning Group. The NPG remains the forum where all member countries (apart from France - due to its decision not to participate), are able to discuss on a broad range of nuclear policy issues. These discussions, along with NATO's nuclear capabilities, follow a clear policy, based on two public documents: the 2022 Strategic Concept, and the 2012 Deterrence and Defence Posture Review. With these documents, the Alliance stressed the fundamental deterrent role played its nuclear forces, and that they will be used only in extreme circumstances, "should the fundamental security of any NATO Ally be threatened", and after consultations in the NPG have been made.[16]

NATO does not seek an arms race, as it is fully committed to arms control, disarmament, and non-proliferation, and it has significantly reduced the number of land-based nuclear weapons in Europe over time. With the war in Ukraine, NATO leaders affirmed their willingness to strengthen the Alliance's deterrence and defence posture, by developing several capabilities ready to be deployed, to maintain a credible deterrence and defence against any adversary. During the Summit in Vilnius in 2023, NATO countries re-emphasised the Alliance's readiness and effectiveness of its nuclear deterrent, aiming at modernising its assets, in order to adapt to the current scenario.[17]

The Alliance aims also at maintaining its military and technological edge, and over the time it has also taken several steps towards the development and modernisation of its capabilities, both in the nuclear and conventional domain. For example, the Alliance is further investing more on defence expenditures through the Defence Investment Pledge, keeping its technological edge through innovations in emerging and disruptive technologies, and implementing initiatives aimed at bringing together governments, the private sector and academia, to keep the Alliance prepared for future challenges.[18] Furthermore, NATO continues to do military

---

[16] "NATO's nuclear deterrence policy and forces", *NATO*, October 20, 2023, https://www.nato.int/cps/en/natohq/topics_210907.htm.
[17] Ibid. See also "Vilnius Summit Communiqué", *NATO*, July 11, 2023, https://www.nato.int/cps/en/natohq/official_texts_217320.htm .

exercises, to make its deterrence and defence posture even more credible, as demonstrated by the annual nuclear exercise, which recently took place (the exercise "Steadfast Noon").[19]

Whilst Russia remains the main challenge for the Alliance, NATO has recognised other security concerns, primarily coming from the People's Republic of China, due to its ongoing military modernisation. Considering the current instability in the global security environment, the PRC will be able to have an impact on NATO's core tasks. Especially considering Beijing's interests over Taiwan, the rise of China as nuclear peer would create a challenge for NATO and the United States in particular, as its nuclear posture and strategy are not designed to counter two nuclear adversaries at the same time. Thus, a stronger nuclear China would have implications for the U.S. extended deterrence, and hence NATO's credibility on deterrence and defence.

II.   The Rise of China in the nuclear domain

Over the past decades, the People's Republic of China has been experiencing "one of the most fundamental transformations observed over the past few decades", that will let Beijing have a major influence in the international arena.[20] The country's GDP has increased exponentially over the past 30 years, and its economic leap has led to a major technological improvement in its capabilities. Considering China's military power, the PRC's defence budget has grown, leading to an extraordinary "shift in terms of quantity and quality of weapons and delivery systems", expanding the country's capabilities in multiple domains.[21] With the 2022 Strategic Concept, NATO Allies showed further concern

---

[18] "Deterrence and defence", *NATO*, October 10, 2023, https://www.nato.int/cps/en/natohq/topics_133127.htm#maintain .

[19] "NATO holds long-planned annual nuclear exercise", *NATO*, October 13, 2023, https://www.nato.int/cps/en/natohq/news_219443.htm?selectedLocal e=en .

[20] Jones, Bruce, "China and the return of great power strategic competition", *Brookings*, February, 2020, https://www.brookings.edu/articles/china-and-the-return-of-great-power-strategic-competition/ .

[21] Gilli, Andrea, Gilli, Mauro, Grgić, Gorana, Henke, Marina, Lanoszka, Alexander, Meijer, Hugo, Scaglioli, Lucrezia, Silove, Nina, Simón, Luis, and Smeets, Max, "Strategic Shifts and NATO's new Strategic Concept", (NATO Defense College, Rome, 2022).

towards the PRC's ambitions, due to its use of "a broad range of political, economic and military tools to increase its global footprint and project power, while remaining opaque about its strategy, intentions and military buildup".[22] This was further emphasised at the Vilnius Summit, in which Allies agreed on being available to have a constructive dialogue with Beijing. Nevertheless, NATO members re-emphasised their concerns, especially considering Beijing's use of hybrid and cyber operations; its confrontational rhetoric and disinformation campaigns; and its aim to "control key technological and industrial sectors, critical infrastructure, and strategic materials and supply chains", using economic leverages and enhance its influence.[23] Especially in the nuclear domain, an increased role for Beijing in the nuclear chessboard will require further attention from other nuclear powers. Indeed, the U.S. Department of Defense (DoD) estimated that the PRC will increase its arsenal, reaching over 1,000 nuclear warheads by 2030, to be deployed at higher readiness levels, and that has already built nearly 300 missile silos in the country's territory.[24] Clearly, this expansion in its nuclear arsenal represents a matter of concern. Furthermore, this expansion is going hand in hand with the PRC's overall military modernisation process, both in quantitative and qualitative terms: as of January 2023 Beijing increased its ICBM launchers to over 450, replacing also older systems with newer ones, characterised by a longer range, and capable of carrying more warheads; similarly, China began the construction of its next-generation SSBNs (nuclear-powered ballistic missile submarines), which are "expected to be larger and quieter [...] and could potentially be equipped with more missile-launch tubes".[25]

b. *Implications*

---

[22] NATO, *2022 Strategic Concept*, para 13.

[23] NATO, Vilnius Summit Communiqué, para 23.

[24] U.S. Department of Defense (U.S. DoD), *Military and Security Developments Involving the People's Republic of China*, October 19, 2023, https://www.defense.gov/Spotlights/2023-China-Military-Power-Report/ .

[25] Kristensen, Hans M., and Korda, Matt, "V. Chinese nuclear forces", *in SIPRI Yearbook 2023: Armaments, Disarmaments and International Security* (Oxford University Press, 2023), p. 293.

Overall, a stronger and more influential China in the international arena will be able to affect NATO and its core tasks, especially that of Defence and Deterrence.[26] Clearly, with an increase in Beijing's military power, driven by its economic growth over the past decades, might portray a transition of power from the Euro-Atlantic area to the Indo-Pacific. From this, it is possible to draw some effects that might have an impact on the balance of power within the international arena. First, China's ongoing modernization in the military domain (both in the nuclear realm, but also in the conventional one) might redirect the United States' major interests towards Asia, lowering its capabilities in Europe, especially considering the nuclear deterrent currently deployed in the old continent. As the current U.S. nuclear deterrence posture and strategy is not designed to tackle two nuclear adversaries at the same time, since NATO's nuclear posture depends on the capabilities of its Allies, mainly the U.S. ones, a further expansion in Beijing's nuclear arsenal clearly affects the Alliance's credibility on deterrence. An example of this switch of scenarios might happen if the situation in Taiwan worsens over time. This increase in the size, readiness, and variety of its arsenal allows "Beijing to initiate wartime escalation without fear that the United States could respond by destroying its nuclear force".[27] Even if it still maintains its "no-first-use policy", China's pattern in the nuclear domain remains a dangerous element to consider. Indeed, a potential conflict over the Taiwan would highly stress the ability of the United States to play multiple roles in Europe and in the Indo-Pacific, affecting the U.S. extended deterrence strategy.[28] "Without Washington's kit, Europeans would likely be outnumbered, and definitely outranged by Moscow's missile force", given the chance for opportunistic behaviours from Russia, if the U.S. will further concentrate its resources in the Indo-Pacific.[29] Thus, it will be important for NATO European

---

[26] Heisbourg, François, "NATO 4.0: the Atlantic Alliance and the rise of China", *Survival*, Vol. 62, No. 2 (2020), pp. 83-102.

[27] Lieber, Keir A., and Press, Daryl G., "The Return of Nuclear Escalation", *Foreign Affairs*, October 24, 2023, https://www.foreignaffairs.com/united-states/return-nuclear-escalation.

[28] Weaver, Gregory, "The role of nuclear weapons in a Taiwan crisis", *Atlantic Council*, November 22, 2023, https://www.atlanticcouncil.org/in-depth-research-reports/issue-brief/the-role-of-nuclear-weapons-in-a-taiwan-crisis/.

countries to develop new strategies, doctrines, and boost their capabilities, to deter Russia in case of a limited support from Washington.

Secondly, a change of focus from the European continent to the Indo-Pacific will require a change in the Alliance's strategy, compromising "European security in general and NATO's conventional defence posture in particular".[30] In fact, being Europe and East Asia two different theatres (being the former composed mainly by land, and the latter of coastal, peninsular, and insular areas), a strategy on Asia will require different capabilities, mainly based on sea and air power, requiring different investments, technologies, and training. Hence, this will reduce the effectiveness of European defence spending dedicated to the European continent, due to the shift of investments towards Asia. [31] Finally, the Chinese technological progress has lowered the costs of many electronic tools in the global market. However, an increased dependence on Chinese products would generate risks and vulnerabilities in the defence sector.[32]

III.   A new phase for Arms Control

The return of great power competition has brought the future of arms control and non-proliferation agreements to the discussion table too.[33] Arms control represents an important tool to increase security, that would help promoting responsible behaviours among countries. However, despite the willingness to adopt limitations on weapons, the treaties that were established since the end of the Cold War are gradually eroding, opening opportunities for further escalation. As of 2023, the war in Ukraine still goes on, and Russia's Duma recently revoked the ratification of the 1996 Comprehensive Test Ban Treaty (CTBT), and suspended its commitments towards the New Strategic Arms Reduction Treaty (New

---

[29] Loss and Mehrer, "Striking absence: Europe's missile gap and how to close it".

[30] Gilli, *et al.*, *Strategic Shifts and NATO's new Strategic Concept*, p. 24.

[31] Ibid.

[32] Woetzel, Jonathan, Lin, Diaan-Yi, Seong, Jeongmin, Madgavkar, Anu, and Lund, Susan, *China's role in the next phase of globalization* (McKinsey Global Institute, San Francisco, CA, 2017). Gansler, Jacques S., *Democracy's arsenal, creating a twenty-first century defense industry* (MIT Press, Cambridge, MA, 2011).

[33] Jankowsky, *NATO and the future of arms control*.

START). Such decisions may represent only the tip of the iceberg, as they "could pave the way for much more radical moves".[34] As for China, Beijing is proceeding with its military build-up, and refuses to join the treaties that are still valid, "until American and Russian arsenals come down in size".[35] For these reasons, it is important to understand what is currently at stake.

a. The state of the art so far

The end of the Cold War marked the beginning a new era in Europe. Countries began to reduce their spending on defence, while U.S. deployed nuclear weapons shrank in numbers.[36] The post-Cold War era also brought the establishment of a new "regional-conventional-arms-control regime", from which the Treaty on Conventional Armed Forces in Europe (CFE) was drafted. Along with this treaty, the 1980s were characterised by a common goal to ensure transparency and to build confidence among countries, provided by another regime of the Vienna Document on Confidence- and Security-Building Measures, and the Treaty on Open Skies. From these agreements, others followed, such as those between the U.S. and Russia as the Strategic Arms Reduction Treaty (START I) or the Strategic Offensive Reductions Treaty (SORT), which both "significantly reduced [the two countries'] stockpiles on non-strategic nuclear weapons".[37] In addition, the INF (Intermediate-Range Nuclear Forces) Treaty of 1987, the U.S. and the Soviet Union decided not to possess missiles with ranges of 500 to 5,000 kilometres. It was the first time that two superpowers agreed to reduce their arsenals, by destroying an entire category of weapons from their stockpiles (they were then followed by other countries).[38] With the

---

[34] Grand, Camille, "Another blow to arms control: Russia's 'de-ratification' of the nuclear test ban treaty", *ECFR*, November 2, 2023, https://ecfr.eu/article/another-blow-to-arms-control-russias-de-ratification-of-the-nuclear-test-ban-treaty/.

[35] Kühn, Ulrich, and Williams, Heather, "A New Approach to Arms Control", *Foreign Affairs*, June 14, 2023 https://www.foreignaffairs.com/united-states/new-approach-arms-control.

[36] NATO, "NATO's nuclear deterrence policy and forces".

[37] Grand, Camille, "Missile, Deterrence and Arms Control: Options for a New era in Europe", *IISS*, September 25, 2023, https://www.iiss.org/research-paper/2023/09/missiles-deterrence-and--arms-control-options--for-a-new-era-in-europe/.

collapse of the Soviet Union, the treaty was applied also to Russia. However, in 2013, the U.S. showed some concern over Moscow's attempt to develop a new type of ground-launched cruise missile (GLCM). Between 2013 and 2019, Washington tried to engage Moscow multiple times, in order to share its non-compliance concerns, until it withdrew the agreement in 2019, due to Russia's violations. This behaviour showed Moscow's intentions to modernize its own nuclear arsenal.[39]

Today, Russia continues its aggression in Ukraine, and it has already withdrawn from the CFE, the New START, INF, and many other treaties. As for China, on the other hand, while expanding its nuclear arsenal it still affirms its policy of No First Use (NFU). Recently, officials representing the U.S. and China met to discuss arms control and non-proliferation issues. However, despite the talks, the meeting did not provide many positive results. Clearly, it will take time before there will be actual negotiations between the U.S. and China on arms control, "as long as China continues to refuse to discuss its growing nuclear arsenal more candidly".[40]

b.   An assessment for the future

Considering the current state of the art of arms control, it might be reasonable to think if there will be any developments in the future, even if the erosion of different treaties over the years does not give much hope.

An important challenge that these negotiations are facing is presented by the capabilities to include in the treaty-to-be. Indeed, costly standoffs between parties, due to their different priorities, represent an important element to consider.[41] On

---

[38] Kimball, Daryl, 'The Intermediate-Range Nuclear Forces (INF) Treaty at a Glance', *Arms Control Association*, August, 2019, https://www.armscontrol.org/factsheets/INFtreaty.

[39] Grand, "Missile, Deterrence and Arms Control: Options for a New era in Europe".

[40] Wiley, Chelsey, and Alberque, William, "Meagre results from the US-China meeting on arms control", *IISS*, November 21, 2023, https://www.iiss.org/online-analysis/missile-dialogue-initiative/2023/10/meagre-results-from-the-us-china-meeting-on-arms-control/ .

[41] Grand, "Missile, Deterrence and Arms Control: Options for a New era in Europe".

that matter, Fearon's analysis on the strategic structure problems within international cooperation shows this kind of issue. According to the author, states must first resolve bargaining problems related to the terms of the negotiation before even implementing the agreement. If a country has high expectations that having further interactions in "the shadow of the future" with the other parties will make enforcing the agreement easier, it will provide further incentives to bargain harder, delaying implementation. Therefore, "the more states value future benefits, the greater the incentive to bargain hard for a good deal, possibly fostering costly standoffs that impede cooperation".[42] With regards to arms control treaties, disputes over which capabilities should be limited or under verification, or destruction, represent an important challenge while bargaining. This is further complicated by the acceleration in the development of new technologies, as "categories defined in previous agreements [...] fall short of addressing new types of delivery systems".[43]

But the debate on the future of arms control also offers some opportunities, that might compensate for the erosion brought by the current challenges in the international arena. An option would be to consider agreements that mainly aim at outlining rules for responsible behaviours. Such agreements will not put actual limits on certain types of weapons, but it "would focus on specific good behaviours, such as notifying others about missile test launches and not relying on hair-trigger alerts".[44] This kind of agreement would foster dialogue among nuclear states, while providing an opportunity to draw clear redlines.[45] Secondly, having a long-standing commitment towards arms control and non-proliferation, NATO might develop a strategy that might open negotiations with Russia and China on arms control, as it did in 1979 with the so-called "Double-Track Decision". Following this strategy, NATO might create a

---

[42] Fearon, James D., "Bargaining, Enforcement, and International Cooperation", *International Organization*, No. 52, Iss. 2 (Spring 1998), pp. 269-305.

[43] Grand, "Missile, Deterrence and Arms Control: Options for a New era in Europe", p.22.

[44] Kühn and Williams, "A New Approach to Arms Control".

[45] Monitz, Ernest J., and Nunn, Sam, "Confronting the New Nuclear Peril", *Foreign Affairs*, April 5, 2023, https://www.foreignaffairs.com/ukraine/russia-confronting-new-nuclear-peril .

dialogue opportunity with the two main nuclear counterparts, but at the same time it will be able to strengthen its deterrent capabilities, should negotiations fail.[46] Finally, another option would be related to the development of new technologies and the challenges they may bring if applied to modern nuclear weapons, it will be important to further consider common agreements that aim at "outlining basic norms and rules for responsible state behaviour".[47] Indeed, the development of Emerging and Disruptive Technologies (EDTs) might have a negative impact, due to the lack of understanding and awareness of the adversaries' EDTs capabilities, or the risk of causing inadvertent escalations, due to miscalculations.[48] Thus, it will be important for future agreements to find measures that will focus "on the most destabilising systems and testing whether the other side is willing to abjure such capabilities through dialogue".[49]

IV.   Conclusions

The war in Ukraine has brought nuclear weapons back to the global political agenda. This new context has prompted NATO to consider new strategies to deter Moscow, but also to adapt itself against the current security environment. The aim of this study was to better understand the role of the Alliance's first pillar of deterrence and defence, emphasising how nuclear weapons represent an essential part of the Alliance's resources for a credible and efficient deterrent. Furthermore, the study aimed to analyse one of the main challenges for the Alliance in making deterrence more credible: Beijing's military modernisation. While Moscow remains the most direct challenge for the Alliance, the PRC's military buildup in the conventional and nuclear domains represents an

---

[46] Maurer, John D., "The Dual-Track Approach: A long-term Strategy for a Post-INF Treaty World", *War on the Rocks*, April 10, 2019, https://warontherocks.com/2019/04/the-dual-track-approach-a-long-term-strategy-for-a-post-inf-treaty-world/ .

[47] Jankowsky, *NATO and the future of arms control*, p. 57.

[48] Kubiak, Katarzyna, and Mishra, Sylvia, "Emerging & disruptive technologies and nuclear weapons decision making: Risks, challenges & mitigation strategies", *European Leadership Network*, December 7, 2021, https://www.europeanleadershipnetwork.org/report/emerging-disruptive-technologies-and-nuclear-weapons-decision-making-risks-challenges-mitigation-strategies/ .

[49] Grand, "Missile, Deterrence and Arms Control: Options for a New era in Europe", p.23.

important challenge for NATO. In the hypothetical scenario of a future conflict over Taiwan, the U.S. will need to compete with two nuclear powers at the same time, transferring more resources into the Indo-Pacific, and thus limiting its extended deterrence efforts over Europe. Moreover, the Chinese technological growth may lead to future vulnerabilities in the cyber domain, in being further dependent on Chinese technologies.

Finally, considering the importance of arms control treaties, this chapter offered a brief analysis of the current prospects for arms control. While it is evident that arms control negotiations with Russia and China are currently narrow, it is still possible to reflect on some of the issues that states might face when dealing with this kind of negotiations. First, it is important to consider the bargaining problems at the core of these agreements. Secondly, NATO might be able to open for a dialogue with Russia and China in the future, by developing a strategy that could emulate the principle of Double-Track Decision. Finally, despite the current difficulties in maintaining an arms control agreement, future strategies should focus on multi-domain solutions, allowing greater flexibility in the approach towards an agreement between the parties involved.

The views expressed in this chapter are the responsibility of the author, and do not necessarily reflect the opinions of NATO, or any other institution represented by the contributor.

Bibliography

Alberque, William, "NATO allies fully suspend implementation of the CFE Treaty", *International Institute for Security Studies (IISS)*, Online Analysis, November 8, 2023, https://www.iiss.org/online-analysis/online-analysis/2023/10/nato-allies-fully-suspend-implementation-of-the-cfe-treaty/ .

Andersson, Jan Joel, "Building Weapons Together (or not)", *European Union Institute for Security Studies (EUISS)*, Brief, November 16, 2023, https://www.iss.europa.eu/content/building-weapons-together-or-not.

Andersson, Jan Joel, "Buying weapons together (or not): Joint defense acquisition and parallel arms procurement", *European Union Institute for Security Studies (EUISS)*, Brief, April 3, 2023, https://www.iss.europa.eu/content/buying-weapons-together-or-not .

Bugos, Shannon, and Masterson, Julia, "New Chinese Missile Silo Fields Discovered", *Arms Control Today*, Arms Control Association, September, 2021 https://www.armscontrol.org/act/2021-09/news/new-chinese-missile-silo-fields-discovered.

Coker, Christoher, "Why NATO should return home. The case for a twenty-first century alliance", *The RUSI Journal*, Vol. 153, No. 4, 2008, pp. 6-11.

Cunningham, Fiona S., and Fravel, M. Taylor, "Assuring assured retaliation: China's nuclear posture and US-China strategic stability", *International Security*, Vol. 40, Iss. 2 (2015), pp. 7-50.

Fearon, James D., "Bargaining, Enforcement, and International Cooperation", *International Organization*, No. 52, Iss. 2 (Spring 1998), pp. 269-305.

Gansler, Jacques S., *Democracy's arsenal, creating a twenty-first century defense industry*, MIT Press, Cambridge, MA, 2011.

Gilli, Andrea, and De Dreuzy, Pierre (edited by), "Nuclear strategy in the 21st century: continuity or change?", *NDC Research Paper,* No. 27, December, NATO Defense College, Rome, 2022.

Gilli, Andrea, and De Dreuzy, Pierre, "Russia's nuclear coercion in Ukraine", *NATO Review*, November 29, 2022, https://www.nato.int/docu/review/articles/2022/11/29/russias-nuclear-coercion-in-ukraine/index.html.

Gilli, Andrea, Gilli, Mauro, Grgić, Gorana, Henke, Marina, Lanoszka, Alexander, Meijer, Hugo, Scaglioli, Lucrezia, Silove, Nina, Simón, Luis, and Smeets, Max, "Strategic Shifts and NATO's new Strategic Concept", *NDC Research Paper,* No. 24, June, NATO Defense College, Rome, 2022.

Grand, Camille, "Another blow to arms control: Russia's 'de-ratification' of the nuclear test ban treaty", *European Council on Foreign Relations (ECFR)*, European Power, November 2, 2023   https://ecfr.eu/article/another-blow-to-arms-control-russias-de-ratification-of-the-nuclear-test-ban-treaty/ .

Grand, Camille, "Missile, Deterrence and Arms Control: Options for a New era in Europe", *International Institute for Security Studies (IISS),* the Missile Dialogue Initiative, Research   Papers,   September   25,   2023, https://www.iiss.org/research-paper/2023/09/missiles-deterrence-and--arms-control-options--for-a-new-era-in-europe/ .

Heisbourg, François, "NATO 4.0: the Atlantic Alliance and the rise of China", *Survival*, Vol. 62, No. 2, 2020, pp. 83-102.

HM Government, "Integrated Review Refresh 2023: Responding to a more contested and volatile world", March 2023, https://assets.publishing.service.gov.uk/government/uploads/system/uploads/attachment_data/file/1145586/11857435_NS_IR_Refresh_2023_Supply_AllPages_Revision_7_WEB_PDF.pdf .

Jankowsky, Dominik P. (edited by), "NATO and the future of arms control"*, NDC Research Paper,* No. 21, NATO Defense College, Rome, 2021.

Jones, Bruce, "China and the return of great power strategic competition", *Brookings*, February, 2020, https://www.brookings.edu/articles/china-and-the-return-of-great-power-strategic-competition/ .

Kimball, Daryl, "The Intermediate-Range Nuclear Forces (INF) Treaty at a Glance", *Arms Control Association*, August, 2019, https://www.armscontrol.org/factsheets/INFtreaty .

Kubiak, Katarzyna, and Mishra, Sylvia, "Emerging & disruptive technologies and nuclear weapons decision making: Risks, challenges & mitigation strategies", *European Leadership Network,* Report, December 7, 2021, https://www.europeanleadershipnetwork.org/report/emerging-disruptive-technologies-and-nuclear-weapons-decision-making-risks-challenges-mitigation-strategies/ .

Kristensen, Hans M., and Korda, Matt, "V. Chinese nuclear forces", in Stockholm International Peace Research Institute (SIPRI), *SIPRI Yearbook 2023: Armaments, Disarmaments and International Security*, pp. 284-293, Oxford University Press, 2023.

Kristensen, Hans M., and Korda, Matt, "Chinese nuclear forces, 2020", *Bulletin of the Atomic Scientists*, Vol. 76, No. 6, 2020, pp. 443-457.

Kühn, Ulrich, and Williams, Heather, "A New Approach to Arms Control", *Foreign Affairs*, June 14, 2023 https://www.foreignaffairs.com/united-states/new-approach-arms-control .

Lieber, Keir A., and Press, Daryl G., "The Return of Nuclear Escalation", *Foreign Affairs*, October 24, 2023, https://www.foreignaffairs.com/united-states/return-nuclear-escalation .

Loss, Rafael, and Mehrer, Angela, "Striking absence: Europe's missile gap and how to close it", *European Council on Foreign Relations (ECFR)*, European Power, November 21, 2023, https://ecfr.eu/article/striking-absence-europes-missile-gap-and-how-to-close-it/ .

Mattelaer, Alexander, "Bleak prospects for nuclear disarmament", *Egmont Institute,* October 30, 2023, https://www.egmontinstitute.be/bleak-prospects-for-nuclear-disarmament/ .

Mattelaer, Alexander, and Verstraete, Wannes, "Why Europe Needs a Nuclear Deterrence Renaissance", *ISPI*, Commentary, June 27, 2022 https://www.ispionline.it/en/publication/why-europe-needs-nuclear-deterrence-renaissance-35568 .

Maurer, John D., "The Dual-Track Approach: A long-term Strategy for a Post-INF Treaty World", *War on the Rocks*, April 10, 2019, https://warontherocks.com/2019/04/the-dual-track-approach-a-long-term-strategy-for-a-post-inf-treaty-world/ .

Monitz, Ernest J., and Nunn, Sam, "Confronting the New Nuclear Peril", *Foreign Affairs*, April 5, 2023, https://www.foreignaffairs.com/ukraine/russia-confronting-new-nuclear-peril .

Moravcsik, Andrew, "5. Armaments Among Allies: European Weapons Collaboration", in Evans, Peter B., Jacobson, Harold K., and Putnam, Robert D. (edited by), *Double-Edged Diplomacy, International Bargaining and Domestic Politics*, pp. 128-167, 1993, University of California Press, United States.

NATO, "Deterrence and defence", *NATO*, October 10, 2023, https://www.nato.int/cps/en/natohq/topics_133127.htm#maintain .

NATO, "NATO holds long-planned annual nuclear exercise", *NATO*, October 13, 2023, https://www.nato.int/cps/en/natohq/news_219443.htm?selectedLocale=en .

NATO, "NATO's nuclear deterrence policy and forces", *NATO*, October 20, 2023, https://www.nato.int/cps/en/natohq/topics_210907.htm .

NATO, "Vilnius Summit Communiqué", *NATO*, July 11, 2023,

https://www.nato.int/cps/en/natohq/official_texts_217320.htm
.

NATO, *NATO 2022 Strategic Concept*, June 29, 2022, https://www.nato.int/nato_static_fl2014/assets/pdf/2022/6/pdf/290622-strategic-concept.pdf .

NATO, "Deterrence and Defence Posture Review", *NATO*, May 20, 2012, https://www.nato.int/cps/en/natohq/official_texts_87597.htm .

Naughtie, Andrew, and Baniya, Sudesh, "Europe's military spending soars, fuelled by Ukraine war", *Euronews*, April 24, 2023, https://www.euronews.com/2023/04/24/europes-military-spending-soars-fuelled-by-ukraine-war.

Pedlow, Gregory W., "NATO strategy documents: 1949-1969", *NATO International Staff Central Archives,* 1999.

Republique Française, "Revue nationale stratégique", *Republique Française,* 2022, https://www.sgdsn.gouv.fr/files/files/Revue%20nationale%20strat%C3%A9gique%20-%20Fran%C3%A7ais.pdf .

Republique Française, "What France achieved", *France TNP*, https://www.francetnp.gouv.fr/what-france-achieved?lang=fr .

Rühle, Michael, "Crisis Management in NATO", *European Security*, Vol. 2, No. 4, 1993, pp. 491-501.

Ruiz-Palmer, Diego, "A strategy odyssey: constancy of purpose and strategy-making in NATO, 1949-2019", *NDC Research Paper*, No. 3, NATO Defense College, Rome, 2019.

Smith, James M., e Bolt, Paul J. (edited by), *China's strategic arsenal: worldview, doctrine, and systems*, Georgetown University Press, Washington, DC, 2021.

Tertrais, Bruno, "Principles of Nuclear Deterrence and Strategy", *NDC Research Paper*, No. 19, May, NATO Defense College, Rome, 2021.

U.S. Department of Defense (U.S. DoD), "Military and Security Developments Involving the People's Republic of

China", *Annual Report to Congress*, October 19, 2023, https://www.defense.gov/Spotlights/2023-China-Military-Power-Report/ .

Vavasseur, Xavier, "France Successfully Test-Fires New M51.3 SLBM", *Naval News*, November 19, 2023, https://www.navalnews.com/naval-news/2023/11/france-successfully-test-fires-new-m51-3-slbm/ .

Wiley, Chelsey, and Alberque, William, "Meagre results from the US-China meeting on arms control", *International Institute for Security Studies (IISS)*, the Missile Dialogue Initiative, November 21, 2023, https://www.iiss.org/online-analysis/missile-dialogue-initiative/2023/10/meagre-results-from-the-us-china-meeting-on-arms-control/ .

Weaver, Gregory, "The role of nuclear weapons in a Taiwan crisis", *Atlantic Council*, November 22, 2023, https://www.atlanticcouncil.org/in-depth-research-reports/issue-brief/the-role-of-nuclear-weapons-in-a-taiwan-crisis/ .

Weaver, Gregory, "The urgent imperative to maintain NATO's nuclear deterrence", *NATO Review*, September 29, 2023, https://www.nato.int/docu/review/articles/2023/09/29/the-urgent-imperative-to-maintain-natos-nuclear-deterrence/index.html .

Woetzel, Jonathan, Lin, Diaan-Yi, Seong, Jeongmin, Madgavkar, Anu, and Lund, Susan, "China's role in the next phase of globalization", *McKinsey Global Institute*, San Francisco, CA, 2017.

Wright, Timothy, "Is China gliding toward a FOBS capability?", *International Institute for Security Studies (IISS)*, Online Analysis, October 22, 2021, https://www.iiss.org/online-analysis/online-analysis/2021/10/is-china-gliding-toward-a-fobs-capability/ .

Zhao, Tong, "It's Time to Talk About No First Use", *Foreign Policy*, November 6, 2023, https://foreignpolicy.com/2023/11/06/united-states-china-nuclear-meeting-no-first-use-arms-control/ .

Giacomo Andolfatto *is currently an assistant at the NATO Defense College (NDC) in Rome. He holds a BA in International Studies from the University of Trento, and a MA in Comparative International Relations from the Ca' Foscari University of Venice, graduating with a dissertation on NATO's potential role in the Sahel region. During his academic career he managed to develop his profile through different experiences, such as a spending a semester studying Peace and Conflict Studies at the university of Malmö (Sweden); becoming a qualified journalist within the Italian Association of Journalists; publishing articles online, including a chapter for the Italian Centre for High Defence Studies (Centro Alti Studi per la Difesa – CASD); and working as an intern at the NATO Defense College, before serving as temporary agent, first with the NDC Research Division as Research Assistant, and then as Assistant to the College's Central Registry. His research interests include: defence and security, nuclear weapons, arms control, and deterrence.*

Russia and Central Asia

The impact of the Rise of China on Russo-Western Relations

Domenico Farinelli

Abstract

This article interrelates Europe's current security crises with the latest transformations in the global balance of power. Specifically, it investigates to what extent the geopolitical competition between China and the United States has influenced Russo-Western relations.

Its core hypothesis is that China's rapid rise in power, coupled with its strong criticism of the US-led global order, encouraged the Kremlin to defend its alleged strategic interests with increasing determination, adopting an ever more aggressive attitude towards NATO and its allies. To test this hypothesis, we will first analyse the key strategic connotations of the rise of China, then the gradual deterioration of Russo-Western relations, and finally the constant improvement of Russo-Chinese relations. Since the latter two phenomena have been developing in parallel, and this is coherent with the main strategic repercussions of China's growth, it can be inferred that a close connection exists between the development of a strong Russo-Chinese *entente* and the widening distance between Russia and the West.

Keywords: Strategy, Power, Geopolitics, China, Russia, United States, Europe, Asia, Eurasia

I. **China's exceptional growth and its impact on the global balance of power**

In recent years, China's exceptional economic growth substantially altered the global balance of power. This primarily occurred to the detriment of Western nations, and according to many observers, it has paved the way for a conflict between China and the United States. Among the theories stressing the importance of power relations in international politics, the Power Transition Theory (PTT) is the most renowned and studied. In essence, it suggests that is more likely for a major war to break out whenever a challenger, typically an emerging country experiencing high rates of economic growth, faces a dominant power unable to grow at the same pace. As the challenger is discontent with the status quo, it may decide to attack the dominant power to rebalance the situation in its favour[50]. Representing the second biggest economy in the world, and being ruled by a communist party that rejects many Western values, China is universally considered the main rival of the US. Looking at Beijing's growth through the lenses of the PTT, a confrontation with Washington appears imminent: between 2000 and 2021, US GDP grew on average by 2%, while the Chinese GDP increased by 9% annually[51]. In other words, if over the last twenty years the US economy has slightly more than doubled, the Chinese one has increased 14-fold.

However, applying the PTT to the China-US case could be highly problematic. One of the most innovative critiques has been advanced in 2018 by the American sinologist Michael Beckley. In an article published on International Security, Beckley states that "power is like love; it is easier to experience than to define or measure" [52]. In his opinion, scholars and policy analysts systematically mismeasure power because they use broad indicators of economic and military

---

[50] Organski, Abramo Fimo Kenneth. World Politics (New York: Alfred A. Knopf, 1958), 1959, American Political Science Review 53, no. 2 (1959): 587-587. DOI:10.1017/S000305540023325X.
[51] World Bank. "World Bank national accounts data, and OECD National Accounts data files," visited on 28/10/2023, retrieved from: https://data.worldbank.org/indicator/NY.GDP.MKTP.KD.ZG.
[52] Beckley, Michael. "The Power of Nations: Measuring What Matters." International Security 43, no. 1 (2018, November 01). https://doi.org/10.1162/isec_a_00328

resources, such as GDP and military spending. These standard indicators tally the wealth and military assets of the studied countries without deducting the numerous costs implied in having a larger population, thus exaggerating the capabilities of some relatively poor but very populous States such as Russia, India, or China. To make a more reliable assessment of each country's real national power, Beckley proposes a rough proxy for net resources that he obtains by combining GDP and GDP per capita[53]. The rationale behind this choice is clear: no nation can sustain a protracted war effort if this implies reducing the citizens' standard of living to a level below subsistence. In this perspective, even though China's GDP is nearly comparable to that of the US in gross terms, Beijing can count on much less real resources to invest in the military sector, and to sustain mobilization in the event of a potential war. Therefore, the country appears still incapable of confronting the US in a direct, open conflict.

Nevertheless, Beijing can undermine the global geostrategic landscape through more indirect means. In particular, the enormous Chinese market already acts as a de facto alternative to the Western markets. At the same time, by implementing a highly pragmatic foreign policy strategy, China avoids applying the sanctions imposed by the US on their geopolitical rivals. Instead, in most cases Beijing actively supports other

---

[53] By multiplying the GDP with the GDP per capita, Beckley devised an index assigning equal importance to a nation's total output and its output-per-individual. Beckley himself acknowledged that this approach cannot address the numerous limitations implied in including the GDP into the calculation. However, by penalising population numbers, it offers a far more accurate representation of a nation's net resources compared to gross indicators. Subsequently, other scholars have developed more sophisticated methods to incorporate per capita wealth-related data into the assessment of national power. Two promising approaches emerged in 2020. The first, published in International Studies Quarterly, introduces the concept of Surplus Domestic Product (SDP). The SDP differentiates between subsistence income, necessary for the population's survival, and the excess income that the State can extract and invest in the military sector (Anders, Fariss, and Markowitz, 2020). The second, reported by the European Journal of International Relations, reexamines the concept of Structural Power and links it to Complex Network Science. By doing so, the author developed the "fitness plus preferential attachment" (FPA) model, which explains why US influence over the international system is enduring despite the substantial loss of strategic advantage over US main competitors, among whom China stands out (Winecoff, 2020).

actors interested in reducing US influence over the international system. Putin's Russia is the most prominent example in that sense.

II.   The U-turn of Russo-Western relations between the 1990s and 2020s

According to the Russian-born political scientist Andrei P. Tsygankov, three distinct macro-phases can be identified within the history of post-soviet Russian foreign policy, each of them being characterised by a specific macro-trend. The first macro-phase (1991-2004) is distinguished by a significant decline of Russia's national power within the context of a unipolar international system led by the US. Throughout this period, Moscow made several attempts to establish mutually beneficial relations with the West, considerably reducing its geopolitical ambitions to this aim. The second macro-phase (2005-2019) is marked by a relative resurgence of Russia's national power and a gradual shift of the global balance of power in favour of a few emerging countries, chiefly China. Amid this timeframe, the outbreak of political-security crises within the post-Soviet space spurred an atmosphere of growing hostility and mistrust between Russia and the Western nations. Finally, during the third macro-phase (2019-present) the Kremlin responded to its deteriorating relations with the West through concrete efforts of strategic self-isolation from the European market[54].

Tsygankov illustrates how post-soviet Russia has based its relations with the West not only on bilateral concessions or setbacks, but also on the evolution of the international system. This helps to explain why Russo-Western relations experienced a U-turn precisely between the first and the second macro-phases. Shortly after the fall of the Soviet Union, the Kremlin lacked viable strategic alternatives to its partnership with the European countries. Consequently, considering potential Western sanction as an unbearable challenge, Moscow self-imposed limited reactions to NATO's eastward enlargement. Since the beginning of the second macro-phase, however, China's growing power and its openness to cooperate with Russia allowed the latter to

---

[54] Tsygankov, Andrei P. Russia's Foreign Policy: Change and Continuity in National Identity, Sixth Edition (2022: Rowman and Littlefield). ISBN1442220007, 9781442220003.

confront the West while avoiding complete international isolation, making the Kremlin far more confident in the pursuit of its own strategic goals.

Additionally, China's rapidly expanding influence deeply concerned the US, imposing a steadfast reorientation of their strategic assets towards Eastern and Southern Asia. Starting from the first Obama administration (2009-2012) Washington has considered these areas as strategically crucial regions to which absolute priority must be accorded, even at the cost of penalizing US presence elsewhere, including Europe[55]. The logic underlying this major geopolitical pivot is captured in the title of a study released by the RAND Corporation: "Russia is a Rogue, not a Peer; China is a Peer, not a Rogue" [56]. While acknowledging that both nations are working to change the geopolitical status quo, RAND's researchers find substantial differences between them. Russia is portrayed as a rogue state rather than a peer competitor because, even if its well-equipped armed forces can still pose a consistent threat to the US interests and security, its limited national power will surely prevent it from dominating the entire international system[57]. Conversely, in consideration of its huge and dynamic internal market, China is described as an almost-equal competitor of the US, potentially capable of reshaping the current world order according to its aims and ambitions[58].

---

[55] Shambaugh, David. "Assessing the US 'Pivot' to Asia." Strategic Studies Quarterly 7, no. 2 (2013): 10–19. http://www.jstor.org/stable/26270763.

[56] Dobbins, James, Howard J. Shatz, and Ali Wyne. "Russia Is a Rogue, Not a Peer; China Is a Peer, Not a Rogue: Different Challenges, Different Responses." RAND Corporation (2019). https://www.rand.org/pubs/perspectives/PE310.html.

[57] The term "Rogue State" entered the US foreign policy discourse immediately after the conclusion of the Cold War. It was meant to designate authoritarian regimes using terrorism as a tool of state policy or trying to develop weapons of mass destruction. As time passed, this definition underwent multiple revisions, yet it still presents all the fundamental attributes of its original meaning (Wilson Center, 2011).

[58] It could be objected that this is just the opinion of a single, albeit well-known and highly regarded, research centre and therefore it cannot be considered an exhaustive analysis of US policies. Nevertheless, Washington's political and institutional apparatus demonstrates to have fully embraced all these concepts, having translated them into official documents, as well as concrete actions. See for instance "The Elements of the China Challenge", released in

By prioritising its confrontation with China, Washington finally persuaded the Kremlin that it was underestimating Russia's national power. Therefore, acting under the assumption that the US would no longer dedicate adequate resources to uphold the security architecture of Eastern Europe, Moscow decided to escalate its attacks against NATO-leaning Ukraine. For the aim of the present study, it is inconsequential whether   Putin's assumption will prove valid or not. What truly matters is that this decision has been taken: whenever a situation is perceived as real, it will produce real consequences.

III.   The evolution of Sino-Russian relations: from rivalry to strategic partnership

During the final phase of the Cold War, relations between the Soviet Union and the People's Republic of China laid in a dire state. In the spring of 1969, the ideological and geopolitical rivalry opposing them escalated into armed clashes along their shared border. As later demonstrated by the study of unclassified documents, on that occasion the two nations came very close to striking each other with nuclear weapons[59]. Over the second half of the 1980s, though, ideology began to play a minor role in shaping the foreign policy of great powers. This marked a pivotal shift in the history of Sino-Russian relations: with Moscow exhibiting less aggressive and more pragmatic behaviour, China became immediately more receptive to Russian *détente* efforts[60]. A process of mutual recognition continued throughout the 1990s, and in July 2001, the two countries inked a first Friendship Agreement aimed at

---

2020 under the Republican Secretary of State Mike Pompeo, and the "National Security Strategy", introduced in 2022 by the Democratic Biden administration. Regardless of the different political affiliations of their authors, both documents reaffirm and elaborate upon most of the ideas put forth in the cited RAND's research (The Policy Planning Staff, Office of the Secretary of State, 2020 and Biden-Harris administration, 2022).

[59] Burr, William. "The Sino-Soviet Border Conflict, 1969: U.S. Reactions and Diplomatic Manoeuvres." National Security Archive Electronic Briefing Book N° 49 (June 12, 2001). https://nsarchive2.gwu.edu/NSAEBB/NSAEBB49/.

[60] Knight, Gregory D. "China's Soviet Policy in the Gorbachev Era." The Washington Quarterly 9, no. 2 (1986): 97-108. DOI: 10.1080/01636608609477356.

fostering bilateral trade and aligning their positions within key international bodies. This pact is of exceptional relevance because it established a clear framework to further develop bilateral cooperation, identifying areas of common interest precisely those of outstanding strategic value: namely, energy, trade, and defence.

Acting accordingly, in October 2004 Gazprom established a strategic partnership with CNPC, China's leading oil company. In July 2007, the Russian Ministry of Industry and Energy authorised the Eastern Gas Program, instructing the construction of a new pipeline linking the immense reserves of the Yakuza region to the Russo-Chinese border - later this infrastructure was ambitiously renamed Power of Siberia. In May 2014, the two countries signed a thirty-year deal worth USD 400 billion for the sale of natural gas. The importance of this event should not be underestimated as a long-term procurement agreement was critical to ensure the economic feasibility of the project and, therefore, it stands as evidence of China's strong commitment to its realization[61]. In 2020, Beijing received the first delivery of natural gas through the Power of Siberia, amounting to roughly 4 billion cubic metres, and it is projected that this quantity could increase up to 38 billion cubic metres by the end of 2023[62].

As for bilateral trade, a report addressed to the Congress of the United States in May 2022 signalled that economic exchanges between Russia and China have grown at an extremely rapid pace, especially after 2014 – the year when Russia unilaterally annexed Crimea, generally considered a major breaking point in Russo-Western relations – and mostly at the expense of the European Union[63]. At first glance, the Russo-Chinese commercial relationship may appear seriously imbalanced: in

---

[61] An, Jaehyung, and Dorofeev, Mikhail, and Zhu, Shouxian. "Development of Energy Cooperation between Russia and China." International Journal of Energy Economics and Policy 10, no. 1 (2019): 134–139. https://www.econjournals.com/index.php/ijeep/article/view/8509

[62] Pao, Jeff. "Power of Siberia 2 to divert Europe-bound gas to China." Asia Times (July 20, 2022), visited on 28/10/2023, retrieved from: https://asiatimes.com/2022/07/power-of-siberia-2-to-divert-europe-bound-gas-to-china/.

[63] Congressional Research Service. "China's Economic and Trade Ties with Russia" (May 24, 2022), visited on 28/10/2023, retrieved from: https://crsreports.congress.gov/product/pdf/IF/IF12120.

2021, trade with China accounted for 18% of Russia's total international exchanges, while Moscow covered only 2% of China's foreign trade. Nonetheless, it must be considered that almost all of Russia's non-oil exports to China are highly strategic, as they concern crucial raw materials such as metals, food, and fertilisers. Ergo, a sudden deterioration of bilateral relations would be extremely costly for both parties, not only for the Kremlin.

Finally, a strategic assessment of the Russo-Chinese relationship cannot ignore the defence sector. The first joint military exercise between the two nations dates to August 2005. Thereafter, combined military drills have been repeated regularly, involving ever more personnel and equipment. The exercise Vostok-2018 (meaning "East" in Russian) drew particular attention from international observers: it was held in proximity to the Chinese border, and it involved approximately 300,000 soldiers, 36,000 vehicles, and 1,000 combat aircraft. Previously, the largest military drill in the history of Russian armed forces was exercise Zapad (meaning "West" in Russian) held in 1981 and involving less than 150,000 men. Instead of feeling threatened by this huge deployment of forces, the Chinese government warmly welcomed the initiative, and China itself directly participated in the exercise with a contingent of 3,500 soldiers – it was the first time that Beijing sent a substantial military force abroad during peacetime[64].

Subsequently, Russo-Chinese relations have gradually surpassed this general *entente* and, as late as February 2022, while meeting in Beijing for the opening ceremony of the Winter Olympic Games, Putin and Xi did not hesitate to label their reciprocal ties as a "Limitless Partnership". By doing so, the two leaders demonstrated an unprecedented degree of mutual trust and support. At present, notwithstanding the ongoing conflict in Ukraine, the two countries are aligned in principle on all the most relevant geopolitical issues, and they closely cooperate across various strategic domains.

---

[64] Carlson, Brian G. "Vostok-2018: Another sign of strengthening Russia-China ties. Not an alliance, but defense cooperation is growing." Stiftung Wissenschaft und Politik 47 (2018). https://www.econstor.eu/handle/10419/256535.

IV.   Conclusion

As evidenced by this study, Russo-Chinese relations are primarily strategic in nature. On one hand, over the last twenty years, Russia has regained strategic autonomy from the West by closely aligning itself with China. Moreover, the Kremlin is currently relying on China's growth and resolution to divert US focus and resources away from Eastern Europe. On the other hand, China appears fully dedicated to deepening its partnership with Moscow, although this clearly contributes to reinforcing Russia's assertiveness against Western nations. As this article has demonstrated, by doing so Beijing is pursuing not only its pragmatic foreign policy agenda,   but also a more subtle geopolitical strategy aimed at indirectly confronting US primacy over the international system.

Bibliography

An, Jaehyung, and Dorofeev, Mikhail, and Zhu, Shouxian. "Development of Energy Cooperation between Russia and China." *International Journal of Energy Economics and Policy* 10, no. 1 (2019): 134–139. https://www.econjournals.com/index.php/ijeep/article/view/85 09

Anders, Therese, Christopher J. Fariss, and Jonathan N. Markowitz. "Bread Before Guns or Butter: Introducing Surplus Domestic Product (SDP)." *International Studies Quarterly* 64, no. 2 (2020): 392–405. https://doi.org/10.1093/isq/sqaa013.

Beckley, Michael. "The Power of Nations: Measuring What Matters." *International Security* 43, no. 1 (2018, November 01). https://doi.org/10.1162/isec_a_00328

Biden-Harris administration. "National Security Strategy" (October 12, 2022), visited on 28/10/2023, retrieved from: https://www.whitehouse.gov/wp-content/uploads/2022/10/Biden-Harris-Administrations-National-Security-Strategy-10.2022.pdf.

Burr, William. "The Sino-Soviet Border Conflict, 1969: U.S. Reactions and Diplomatic Manoeuvres." *National Security Archive Electronic Briefing* Book N° 49 (June 12, 2001). https://nsarchive2.gwu.edu/NSAEBB/NSAEBB49/.

Carlson, Brian G. "Vostok-2018: Another sign of strengthening Russia-China ties. Not an alliance, but defense cooperation is growing." *Stiftung Wissenschaft und Politik* 47 (2018). https://www.econstor.eu/handle/10419/256535.

Congressional Research Service. "China's Economic and Trade Ties with Russia" (May 24, 2022), visited on 28/10/2023, retrieved from: https://crsreports.congress.gov/product/pdf/IF/IF12120.

Dobbins, James, Howard J. Shatz, and Ali Wyne. "Russia Is a Rogue, Not a Peer; China Is a Peer, Not a Rogue: Different Challenges, Different Responses." *RAND Corporation* (2019). https://www.rand.org/pubs/perspectives/PE310.html.

Kindred Winecoff, William. "The persistent myth of lost hegemony, revisited: structural power as a complex network phenomenon." *European Journal of International Relations* 26, no. 1_suppl (2020): https://doi.org/10.1177/1354066120952876.

Knight, Gregory D. "China's Soviet Policy in the Gorbachev Era." *The Washington Quarterly* 9, no. 2 (1986): 97-108. DOI: 10.1080/01636608609477356.

Organski, Abramo Fimo Kenneth. *World Politics* (New York: Alfred A. Knopf, 1958), 1959, *American Political Science Review* 53, no. 2 (1959): 587-587. DOI:10.1017/S000305540023325X.

Pao, Jeff. "Power of Siberia 2 to divert Europe-bound gas to China." *Asia Times* (July 20, 2022), visited on 28/10/2023, retrieved from: https://asiatimes.com/2022/07/power-of-siberia-2-to-divert-europe-bound-gas-to-china/.

Shambaugh, David. "Assessing the US 'Pivot' to Asia." *Strategic Studies Quarterly* 7, no. 2 (2013): 10–19. http://www.jstor.org/stable/26270763.

The Policy Planning Staff, Office of the Secretary of State. "The Elements of the China Challenge" (November 2020, Revised December 2020), visited on 28/10/2023, retrieved from: https://www.state.gov/wp-content/uploads/2020/11/20-02832-Elements-of-China-Challenge-508.pdf.

Tsygankov, Andrei P. *Russia's Foreign Policy: Change and Continuity in National Identity*, Sixth Edition (2022: Rowman and Littlefield). ISBN1442220007, 9781442220003.

Wilson Center. ""Rogue States" and the United States: A Historical Perspective" (2011), visited on 28/10/2023, retrieved from: https://www.wilsoncenter.org/event/rogue-states-and-the-united-states-historical-perspective.

World Bank. "World Bank national accounts data, and OECD National Accounts data files," visited on 28/10/2023, retrieved from: https://data.worldbank.org/indicator/NY.GDP.MKTP.KD.ZG.

Domenico Farinelli – *Currently working at the Egmont Royal Institute for International Relations, Domenico Farinelli is a young, talented expert in International Politics. His interests centre around, but are not limited to, Geopolitics, Strategy and Global Governance. In July 2020, he graduated cum laude in International Studies at the University of Trento. In May 2023 he graduated again with top marks, earning a master's degree in International Relations and European Studies from the University of Florence. Before joining the Egmont Institute, Domenico worked as a researcher for FINABEL, an international organization based in Brussels and focused on defence standardization in Europe. From January to June 2024, he is set to assume the role of a Liaison Officer for the Belgian Presidency of the EU.*

Rosvgardia's coup-proofing function within the Russian Federation

Jovan Knezevic

Abstract

A few weeks after Wagner's mutiny, the President of the Russian Federation, Vladimir Putin, signed a decree that authorized the transfer of "heavy" weapons to the National Guard of Russia, (Rosvgardia in Russian). The National Guard is a special force created in 2016 by President Putin to protect the regime from "color revolutions" and coups d'état. The agency counts some 400,000 security personnel, reports directly to the President of Russia, and is led by Putin's longtime friend, Viktor Zolotov. In light of Wagner's armed insurrection, the purpose of this essay is to delve into Rosvgardia's role as Putin's "praetorian guard", analyzing the different ways in which this agency protects the regime from coups d'état.

Key words: Russian Federation, Coup, Coupproofing, Civil-Military Relations, Wagner

I.   Introduction

In June 2023, the mercenaries of the Wagner private military company, led by Evgenij Prigozin, launched an armed mutiny after a period of heightened tensions with the Russian military elites. After the seizure of governmental and military headquarters in Rostov-on-Don, Wagner troops advanced through the Voronezh Oblast towards Russia's capital, encountering little to no armed resistance by the Russian regular army and special forces. In fact, the Russian military suffered significant human and material losses trying to stop Wagner's advance. In the end, Wagner's operation was called off some 200 kilometers from Moscow after less than two days from its launch[1] (See figure 1).   Despite its limited duration, Wagner's mutiny has been described by international media as "the biggest threat the President has faced in his 22-year rule"[2]. The incident fueled Putin's fears about possible coups that could destabilize Russia from within in a moment in which the country's political, economic, and military efforts are devoted to supporting the military campaign in Ukraine.

In an attempt to increase internal security and discourage further coup attempts or popular uprisings, in July 2023, President Putin, signed a decree that authorized the transfer of "heavy equipment" to the National Guard (NG), or *Rosvgardia*[3]. The National Guard is a security agency led by Putin's longtime friend and personal bodyguard, Colonel-General Viktor Zolotov. The agency, which counts around 400.000 military personnel, was created in 2016 to allegedly fight terrorism and extremism, protect national borders and ensure internal security by collaborating with other agencies within the Russian Federation[4]. However, because of its

---

[1] Al Jazeera, "Timeline: How Wagner Groups' revolt against Russia unfolded", June 2023, https://www.aljazeera.com/news/2023/6/24/timeline-how-wagner-groups-revolt-against-russia-unfolded

[2] Al Jazeera, "Timeline: How…"

[3] Sinead Baker, "Russia's 200,000 strong national guard is getting armed with heavy weaponry, in a sign of its growing importance to Putin, UK intel says", Business Insider, Aug 8 2023, https://www.businessinsider.com/russia-national-guard-getting-heavy-weapons-defend-putin-uk-intel-2023-8?r=US&IR=T

[4] Center for Strategic and International Studies, "Rosgvardiya: hurtling towards confrontation?", Sep 2020, https://www.csis.org/blogs/post-soviet-post/rosgvardiya-hurtling-towards-confrontation

ambiguous legal mandate and direct subordination to the President, most analysts regard *Rosvgardia* as a "catch-all force for Putin for whatever hot issue may arise"[5], including coups and protests. In light of Wagner's armed insurrection in June and the recent decision by President Putin to equip the agency with heavy weapons, the purpose of this essay is to discuss the role *Rosvgardia* plays in protecting President Putin and his regime from potential coups d'état.

For analytical purposes, the essay will be divided as follows: in the first section, I will analyze the "statutory" functions of the National Guard along with the socio-political context in which it was created as well as the reasons behind the creation of the agency, arguing that the main driver behind the establishment of the *Rosvgardia* was Putin's need to create a large, loyal special-purpose force that could protect him from protests and coups. Moving on, in the second section, I will briefly describe the agency's structure and leadership while, in the third section, I will discuss *Rosvgardia* 's role within the Russian coercive apparatus in preventing and dealing with coups. I will analyze both the direct and indirect ways in which the agency protects the regime from putsches. Finally, in the last section, I will devote attention to *Rosvgardia*'s limited response during Wagner's armed rebellion. The argument I put forward is that the agency's troops' limited role during Wagner's mutiny was not due to "mass defections" but rather to the lack of heavy military equipment necessary to stop Wagner's advance.

---

[5] Center for Strategic and International Studies, "Rosvgardiya…"

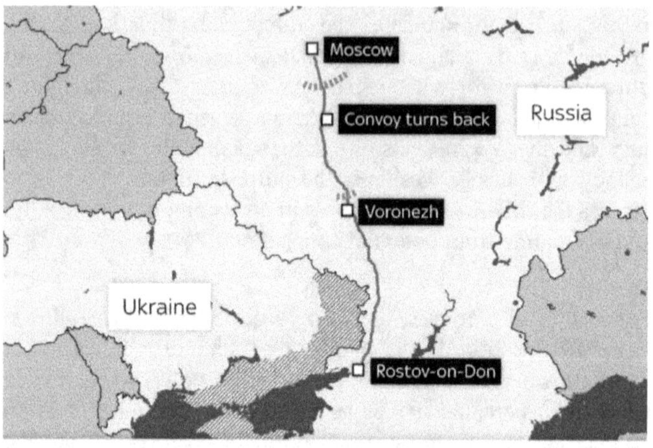

Figure 1: Wagner's advance towards Moscow on June 23 2023[6]

II.   Creation and functions

President Vladimir Putin created the *Rosgvardia* by means of a Presidential Decree in 2016[7]. The stated and "official" reason for the creation of this new security agency was the need to increase security within the Russian Federation. This could be easily inferred from the "On National Guard Troops" bill, in which all the functions of the *Rosvgardia* are listed[8]. According to the bill, the functions of the agency include, but are not limited to: the protection of law and order in collaboration with the police, the fight against terrorism/extremism, the protection of governmental premises, the defense of national territory and the assistance to border guards to protect the state border[9]. Based on its functions, one can argue that the agency has both a "policing" (protecting public order, critical facilities) and a military role (countering terrorism, extremism, and other non-military threats to

---

[6] Sky News 24, "Russia Rebellion: Wagner Group troops to be absorbed into Russian military as mercenary boss Yevgeny Prigozhin heads to Belarus", June 25 2023, https://news.sky.com/story/russia-rebellion-wagner-group-troops-to-be-absorbed-into-russian-military-as-mercenary-boss-yevgeny-prigozhin-heads-to-belarus-12909128

[7] Timothy L. Thomas, *Kremlin Kontrol: Russia's Political-Military Reality* (Fort Leavenworth: Foreign Military Studies Office, 2017), 9

[8] Jolanta Darczewska, "Rosgvardiya: a special-purpose force", (Warsaw: Point of View, Center for Eastern Studies, 2020), p. 10

[9] Jolanta Darczewska, "Rosgvardiya…"

security)[10]. Although the agency was created to perform tasks related to internal security, the *Rosvgardia* was also deployed in theaters abroad: in Crimea, Syria and more recently in Ukraine. In the case of the Kremlin's "special operation" in Ukraine, *Rosvagardia*'s units were initially sent to occupy captured territories; however, their lack of adequate training for fighting inter-state wars combined with Ukraine's fierce resistance, resulted in heavy losses that led to their relocation[11].

Apart from its "official", statutory tasks, the agency fulfils certain "unofficial" functions. Indeed, most analysts tend to consider the *Rosvgardia* as a special force intended to protect Putin and the country's political elites from revolutions and coups d'état. According to Aleksandr Sukharenko, the establishment of the *Rosgvardia* responded to the need to create a "pro-presidential army for the regime's protection from malcontents or color revolutions"[12]. The timing of the creation of the *Rosvgardia* was suggestive in this sense; the establishment of the agency coincided with a moment in which Putin's fears about a possible Russian "color revolution" such as the 2003 "rose revolution" in Georgia, the 2004 "orange revolution" in Ukraine, or the 2005 "tulip revolution" in Kyrgyzstan[13], were reawakened. However, the toppling of President Janukovic in 2014 in Ukraine after the Maidan revolution was particularly instructive; in Putin's view, Ukraine's former President and his government were overthrown as a result of popular uprisings that were fueled by the "West". Therefore, to avoid the destiny of his Ukrainian counterpart, President Putin created a new, loyal security force, directly reporting to him and large enough to defend him from a possible revolution.

In Sukharenko's perspective, the creation of the agency also reflected "the president's distrust of the heads of other special services in case of a coup"[14]. A similar view is shared by

---

[10] Jolanta Darczewska, "Rosgvardiya.."

[11] Alec Bertina, "The Rosgvardia (National Guard of Russia): Russia's internal guard", Grey Dynamics, July 2023, https://greydynamics.com/the-rosgvardia-national-guard-of-russia-putins-internal-guard/

[12] Thomas, *Kremlin control..*, 10

[13] Marvin Kalb, "Why Putin needs a praetorian guard", Brookings, May 2017, https://www.brookings.edu/articles/why-putin-needs-a-praetorian-guard/

Andrey Pertsey, who argued that "the Praetorians were to become a counterweight to the classic security agencies: the Interior Ministry and the Ministry of Defense"[15]. Indeed, while the last military coup in the Russian Federation prior to the creation of the *Rosvgardia* dates back to 1991, coups can never be ruled out in an authoritarian regime. This is particularly the case in times of political upheaval or widespread malcontent. The establishment of the agency thus reflects Putin's attempt to coup-proof his regime, a phenomenon I will analyze in the third section.

Apart from the timing of the creation of the agency, other factors seemed to suggest Putin's intention to use the *Rosvgardia* as a "catch-all force for whatever issue may arise"[16]. According to Bruetsch, two aspects were suggestive in this respect; the first was that the *Rosvgardia* duplicated most of the tasks already performed by the Ministry of Interior (MDV) and other security agencies, questioning the utility of the creation of this new force[17]. A second aspect had to do with the agency's ambiguous legal mandate and lack of oversight mechanism over its actions. This would allow Putin to use the *Rosvgardia* to fight any domestic threat including political opponents and tighten his grip on power[18].

III.   Structure and composition

The structure of the National Guard consists of security forces that had already existed before its creation in 2016. To establish a new security agency these troops were reorganized in what analysts described as "the biggest shake-up of security services in decades"[19]. The most important example of this reorganization was the transfer of 140.000 Internal Troops of the Ministry of Internal Affairs to the newly established *Rosvgardia*. Alongside the transfer of Internal troops, there was also the incorporation of 40.000 from the Special Purpose

---

14 Thomas, *Kremlin control..*, 10

15 Andrey Pertsev, "Putin's head of guard", Riddle, Sep 5 2023, https://ridl.io/putin-s-head-of-guard/

16 Center for Strategic and International Studies, "Rosvgardiya…"

17 Nickolas Bruetsch, "Я, СИЛОВИК ROSGVARDIYA: the emperor's new guards", The Security Distillery, Oct 2021, https://thesecuritydistillery.org/all-articles/-rosgvardiya-the-emperors-new-guards

18 Nickolas Bruetsch, "Я, СИЛОВИК.."

19 Nickolas Bruetsch, "Я, СИЛОВИК.."

Mobile personnel (Otrjad Mobilnii Osobnogo Naznacenija, OMON) and 12.000 personnel from the Specialized Quick Reaction Forces (Specialnyj Otrjad Bystrogo Reagirovanja, SOBR) into the agency. More recently, the special units of the Russian Federal Drug Control Service were transferred to the control of the National Guard as well. According to estimates, the total personnel of the *Rosvgvardia* amounted to 340.000 by 2016, and 400.000 by 2021, although the exact number is unknown. From a territorial point of view, the National Guard is organized into eight districts (Central, Northwest, North Caucasus, Volga, Ural, Eastern and Southern districts) which correspond to the eight federal districts of the Russian Federation[20]. Within the different districts there are directorates at the level of republics, oblasts and units[21].

In terms of leadership, the agency largely consists of conservative men who served in other security institutions within the Russian Federation[22]. For instance, Deputy and State Secretary Colonel-General Oleg Plokhoy, had served in the Federal Security Service for 13 years before joining the *Rosvgardia*[23]. Meanwhile, first deputy Colonel-General Victor Strigunov and the Chief of Staff, Colonel-General Sergey Chechnik had served in the MVD for more than 37 and 40 years, respectively[24]. Last but not least, the director of the agency, Viktor Zolotov, had served in a several positions within Russia's security apparatus before being appointed as head of the security agency. He began his career in the 1970s in the 9th Directorate of the KGB and, after the collapse of the Soviet Union, he worked as a bodyguard in the Main Directorate of Security of the Russian Federation, where he met Putin. Then, between 2003 and 2013 he held the position of Head of the Security Service of the President of the Russian Federation before he became Deputy Commander-in-Chief of the Internal Troops of the MVD in 2013. In 2014, he was appointed as First Deputy Minister of Internal Affairs[25]. The professional homogeneity of the top leadership creates an environment permeated by conservativism and uniformity

---

[20] Jolanta Darczewska, "Rosgvardiya.."
[21] Jolanta Darczewska, "Rosgvardiya.."
[22] Center for Strategic and International Studies, "Rosvgardiya…"
[23] Center for Strategic and International Studies, "Rosvgardiya…"
[24] Center for Strategic and International Studies, "Rosvgardiya…"
[25] Alec Bertina, "The Rosgvardia…"

where loyalty to superiors and the preservation of the status quo are the rule[26].

<h3 style="text-align:center">IV.   Putin's "praetorian guard": Rosvgardia's role in preventing coups d'etat</h3>

As already discussed, *Rosvgardia* is regarded by most analysts and experts as Putin's "praetorian guard": a special and loyal force, independent from the military and carefully policed to protect the regime from internal threats. Indeed, it can be argued that the creation of the National Guard falls within Putin's coup-proofing strategies. Coup-proofing refers to the set of measures authoritarian leaders implement to discourage coups by the military or affect their outcomes. James T. Quinlivan, in his seminal article *"Coup-proofing: its practices and consequences in the Middle East"*, provided a list of coup-proofing tactics commonly adopted by autocrats to prevent military coups. These include:

1. the exploitation of family, ethnic and religious loyalties for coup-critical-positions,
2. the creation of an armed force parallel to the military,
3. the development of multiple internal security agencies with overlapping jurisdictions that constantly monitor the loyalty of the military,
4. the fostering of military expertise in the army,
5. the financing of such measures.[27]

These measures tend to be implemented in tandem; rarely does an autocrat resort to only one as this would be ineffective to coup-proof the regime. In the case of Russia, President Putin has adopted most of them, albeit each to a different extent. In this section, I will analyze both the direct and indirect ways in which the *Rosvardia* protects the regime from coups.

Firstly, the National Guard can play an active role in affecting the outcome of a coup by protecting the regime through special units stationed close to key governmental premises. As many analysts and scholars argue, coups are characterized by the rapid seizure of some symbolical centers of power such as the Parliament or, when possible, the executive him/herself[28].

---

[26] Center for Strategic and International Studies, "Rosvgardiya…"

[27] James T. Quinlivan, "Coup-proofing: its practice and consequences in the Middle East", International Security 24, no. 2 (Fall, 1999): 133

According to Mark Galeotti, expert in Russian security affairs, "With coups, the key issue is how many men can you get quickly into the right positions. Momentum is perhaps the most important…attribute of a successful seizure of power"[29]. To prevent this, the National Guard has some 20,000 personnel deployed in the outskirts of Moscow: the 2nd Guards Tamanskaya Motor Rifle Division and the 4th Guards Kantemirovskaya Tank Division[30]. Moreover, the *Rosvgardia* has another 35.000 armed from the Interior Troops and 35.000 from the OMON, stationed in Moscow[31]. These specialized units within the agency received specific training to defend the regime. In the Zaslon-2021 exercise, for instance, the *Rosvgardia* held small-scale, individual exercises focused on domestic scenarios such as neutralizing enemies in buildings or rescuing hostages[32]. On that occasion, the forces under the agency's command demonstrated capabilities that could be compared to those of the regular army which "indicate(d) that Putin likely intends Rosvgardia to have combat capabilities comparable to those of the regular Russian military"[33]. The National Guard, however, is not the only force guarding the Kremlin. Indeed, the Kremlin is protected by 5.500 armed men from the FSO's Presidential Regiment, a special unit that ensures the security of the Presidency of Russia, as well as 5.000 personnel from the Presidential Guard Service (SBP)[34]. The SBP is a federal governmental agency whose task is to protect the President and the Prime Minister of Russia along with their respective families. In case of a coup, all these units, including the *Rosvgardia*, would physically protect the regime, preventing the seizure of governmental buildings by

---

[28] Erica De Bruin, "Preventing Coups d'ètat", The Journal of Conflict Resolution, 62, no. 7 (August 2018): 1436

[29] Mark Galeotti, "What Turkey can learn from Russia about coup-proofing the military", War on the Rocks, Aug 2 2016, https://warontherocks.com/2016/08/what-turkey-can-learn-from-russia-about-coup-proofing-the-military/

[30] Mark Galeotti, "What Turkey…"

[31] Mark Galeotti, "What Turkey…"

[32] Catherine Hodgson, Will Baumgardner, Mason Clark, "Russian National Guard (Rosvardia) demonstrates new capabilities in first-ever strategic exercise", Institute for the Study of War, August 17 2021, https://www.understandingwar.org/backgrounder/russian-national-guard-rosgvardia-demonstrates-new-capabilities-first-ever-strategic

[33] Catherine Hodgson, Will Baumgardner, Mason Clark, "Russian National Guard…"

[34] Mark Galeotti, "What Turkey…"

conspirators. The presence of specialized units in the vicinity of the Kremlin can also have a "deterrent" effect, discouraging coups in the first place. Indeed, as Mark Galeotti put it, "no one launches a coup unless they think it has a good chance of success"[35].

Secondly, the *Rosvgardia* can also play an indirect role in preventing coups by eliminating one of the causes that push the military to stage a coup in the first place. History is full of examples of militaries defecting and staging coups because they are ordered to use force against their own population. This is particularly true, Lutterbeck argues, when the military is based on general conscription and therefore has a strong relation with the population[36], as in the case of Russia. In Lutterbeck's perspective, when the army is reflective of society as a whole, it will be less inclined to use force against its own population and may be motivated to defect if forced to do so[37]. However, since the task of dealing with internal riots and popular uprisings within the Russian Federation was assigned to the *Rosvgardia*, it could be argued that this agency plays an indirect role in preventing coups d'état by removing one of the causes that encourage military putsches[38].

According to some analysts, there is another indirect way through which *Rosvgardia* fulfills its coup-proofing function. In their perspective, the presence of the National Guard as well as other "counterweight" agencies within the Russian coercive apparatus could negatively affect the outcome of a coup by creating obstacles to communication and coordination in the active phase of the putsch[39]. This is particularly the case if we consider that coups are akin to military operations that require effective and timely coordination and communication among the different actors involved[40]. In Russia, however, the

---

[35] Mark Galeotti, "What Turkey…"

[36] Derek Lutterbeck, "Arab Uprisings, Armed Forces and Civil.Military Relations..", Armed Forces and Society, 39, vol 1 (Apr 2012): 33

[37] Derek Lutterbeck, "Arab Uprisings..", 33

[38] Adam E. Casey, "Putin has coup-proofed his regime", Foreign Policy, March 23 2022, https://foreignpolicy.com/2022/03/23/putin-coup-russian-regime/

[39] Zack Beauchamp, "Could Putin actually fall?", Vox, March 13 2022, https://www.vox.com/22961563/putin-russia-ukraine-coup-revolution-invasion

[40] Erica De Bruin, "Preventing…", 1437

military/security establishment is fragmented into multiple agencies: the *Rosvagrdia*, the Federal Protective Service and the Federal Security Service[41]. Each agency has a separate chain of command and a separate channel for communicating with the regime. Such a highly fragmented coercive apparatus would thus result in a "coordination dilemma" that could hamper effective and timely communication and coordination between the army and other actors within the Russian coercive apparatus[42]. According to Erica De Bruin, on the other hand, the fragmentation of the security service does not affect coups by creating obstacles to coordination and communication. On the contrary, based on evidence from sixteen cases, De Bruin argues that "counterbalancing prevents successful coups largely because counterweights use force to defend incumbent regimes, rather than by creating barriers to coordination and communication between forces"[43]. Hence, contrary to the arguments presented by Casey, Gale and other analysts, the fragmentation of the security service in the case of the Russian Federation will not necessarily lead to "coordination dilemmas". In fact, the seizure of governmental and military headquarters in Rostov-on-Don by the mercenaries led by Prigozhin in the first hours of the mutiny seems to contradict Casey, Gale and other analysts' arguments. However, one should also consider that governmental and military premises in Rostov-on-Don are "tactically" irrelevant for coup-related purposes and are far less protected than those located in Russia's capital.

V. Rosvgardia's role during (and after) Wagner's rebellion

Although the National Guard's primary task is to deal with domestic threats, the role it played during Wagner's armed insurrection in June 2023 was limited. Commenting on the events that unfolded between June 23 and 24, the director of *Rosvgardia*, Viktor Zolotov, claimed that his forces did an excellent job during the mutiny. President Putin, for his part, thanked the forces under Zolotov's command for protecting the capital from turmoil and "preventing a civil war". Some information available online seem to confirm that the Kremlin mobilized the Russian National Guard to barricade the capital

---

[41] Adam E. Casey, "Putin has coup-proofed…"
[42] Zack Beauchamp, "Could Putin…"
[43] Erica De Bruin, "Preventing…", 1452

and stop the entry of Wagner's convoy into Moscow[44]. However, there is no evidence suggesting that the National Guard contributed to effectively stopping Wagner's march toward the capital. Several reasons can explain *Rosvgardia* 's limited role during Wagner's mutiny. According to some analysts, National Guard troops were ordered not to engage Wagner's troops in order not to escalate the situation further[45]. Some images available online, on the contrary, show *Rosvgardia* personnel alongside Wagner units during the seizure of the South Military District. While this may suggest that some of the personnel of the National Guard may have defected to Wagner[46], there is not enough reliable information to draw such conclusions. Another reason could be Wagner's troops' decision to stop the advance 200 km from Russia's capital. If Wagner troops had advanced closer to Moscow, an armed response would, perhaps, have been necessary to protect the Kremlin and the President from a potential coup. However, the most likely reason behind the agency's limited role during the mutiny had to do with the fact that *Rosvgardia* lacked the heavy equipment that would have been necessary to repel Wagner's advance[47]. Wagner mercenaries had received a large amount of military equipment from the Russian military in order to fight alongside the Russian forces in Ukraine. These include tanks and BMP-2/3s, tube artillery pieces, multiple-launch rocket systems, air defense systems and fixed-wing aircraft[48]. As a result, had *Rosvgardia* troops received orders to stop Wagner's advance, they would have to face a much heavier force. This hypothesis seems plausible also considering President Putin's decision to transfer heavy weapons to the National Guard few weeks after the mutiny. Indeed, according to experts, the armed insurrection by the para-military group showed some of the shortcomings of the *Rosvgardia* in terms of combat capabilities and encouraged Putin to transfer heavy weapons to the agency[49]. These include

---

[44] John Psaropoulous, "As Wagner troops marched on Moscow, Ukraine made further gains", Al Jazeera, June 28 2023, https://www.aljazeera.com/news/2023/6/28/as-wagner-troops-marched-on-moscow-ukraine-made-further-gains

[45] Alec Bertina, "The Rosgvardia…"

[46] Alec Bertina, "The Rosgvardia…"

[47] John Hardie, "Russia's National Guard to Get Tanks Following Wagner Mutiny", Long war Journal, June 29 2023, https://www.longwarjournal.org/archives/2023/06/russias-national-guard-to-get-tanks-following-wagner-mutiny.php

[48] John Hardie, "Russia's National…"

tanks, aircrafts, artillery, and warships[50]. Along with the transfer of heavy weapons, it was also announced that special units of the Russian Federal Drug Control Service (GROM) would be incorporated into the *Rosvgardia*. Established within the Federal Human Trafficking Control Service, GROM units are composed of well-trained officers with combat experience in a number of agencies (FSB, SVR and GRU) and the Interior Ministry[51]. The incorporation of GROM units into the National Guard will increase the total number of security personnel under the agency's command, which, according to 2021 estimates amounted to 400.000.

Overall, both the transfer of heavy military equipment and the incorporation of GROM units are intended to increase *Rosvgardia*'s capacity to deal with threats to domestic security and therefore, demonstrate that "President Putin…is solidifying the Russian National Guard's position as a key element in maintaining internal security in Russia"[52].

V.　　Conclusion

In this essay, I discussed *Rosvgardia*'s role in defending President Putin from a potential coup within the Russian Federation. The agency plays an active role in protecting the regime from potential coups through special units stationed in the vicinity of the Kremlin. In case of a coup, these special units would physically protect governmental premises and prevent the seizure of symbolic centers of power by conspirators. Apart from affecting the outcome of a coup, the presence of around 100,000 security personnel is also likely to deter putsch attempts in the first place by decreasing their likelihood of being successful. Moreover, I analyzed the ways in which Rosvgardia indirectly protects the regime from putsches. I described two main strategies in this respect. Firstly, the National Guard plays an indirect role in preventing

---

[49] Army Recognition, "Russian National Guard granted authority to arm personnel with heavy weapons", Aug 9 2023, https://www.armyrecognition.com/defense_news_august_2023_glob al_security_army_industry/russian_national_guard_granted_authority _to_arm_personnel_with_heavy_weapons.html

[50] Alec Bertina, "The Rosgvardia…"

[51] Grzegorz Kuczynski, "Rosvgardia receives heavy weaponry after Wagner's failed rebellion", Warsaw Institute, July 20 2023, https://warsawinstitute.org/rosgvardia-receives-heavy-weaponry-wagners-failed-rebellion/

[52] Army Recognition, "Russian National…"

coups by removing one of the causes that encourage the military to rebel against political authorities. Indeed, when the military has a special relation with the population because it is based on general conscription as in the case of Russia, it is less inclined to use force against the people to quell protests or revolution. If ordered to do so, the army (or part of it), under certain conditions, may be encouraged to mount a coup. In the case of the Russian Federation, however, the primary responsibility for dealing with protests or revolution was given to the *Rosvgardia,* thereby reducing the likelihood that the army will attempt to challenge the regime. Secondly, the presence of multiple security agencies, including the *Rosvgardia* can create obstacles to coordination and communication between the different actors involved in the coup. Since coups are akin to military operations and are based on momentum, this coordination dilemma could, according to some analysts, affect its outcomes.

After having analyzed the different ways in which the National Guard prevents coups d'état in Putin's Russia, I devoted some attention to the role the agency played during Wagner's mutiny in June 2023. Based on information available online, one can conclude that *Rosvagrdia* troops played a limited role during the armed insurrection by the paramilitary groups. While different hypotheses were advanced, the most likely reason behind *Rosvgardia*'s inaction was the lack of heavy equipment necessary to stop Wagner's advance. The decision to transfer heavy weapons to the agency a few weeks after the event supports this hypothesis.

Overall, it can be argued that the National Guard of Russia plays a central role in defending the Kremlin from potential coups d'état. While not being the only security force within the country, Putin's consistent strengthening of its capabilities suggests the centrality of this agency in protecting the regime from potential putsches. The recent decisions by President Putin to transfer heavy weapons to the *Rosvgardia* and provide for the incorporation of GROM units into it, indicate that the agency will play a prominent role in protecting the regime from coups or large-scale protests in the future. The strengthening of National Guard's capabilities will be particularly relevant as the war in Ukraine goes on. Indeed, the increase in the number of casualties among the Russian military, the lowering of soldiers' morale and the economic costs of the war could, at one point, encourage defections or coups within the Russian military establishment.

Bibliography

Adam E. Casey, "Putin has coup-proofed his regime", Foreign Policy, March 23 2022, https://foreignpolicy.com/2022/03/23/putin-coup-russian-regime/

Al Jazeera, "Timeline: How Wagner Groups' revolt against Russia unfolded", June 2023, https://www.aljazeera.com/news/2023/6/24/timeline-how-wagner-groups-revolt-against-russia-unfolded

Alec Bertina, "The Rosgvardia (National Guard of Russia): Russia's internal guard", Grey Dynamics, July 2023, https://greydynamics.com/the-rosgvardia-national-guard-of-russia-putins-internal-guard/

Andrey Pertsev, "Putin's head of guard", Riddle, Sep 5 2023, https://ridl.io/putin-s-head-of-guard/

Army Recognition, "Russian National Guard granted authority to arm personnel with heavy weapons", Aug 9 2023, https://www.armyrecognition.com/defense_news_august_2023_global_security_army_industry/russian_national_guard_granted_authority_to_arm_personnel_with_heavy_weapons.html Catherine Hodgson, Will Baumgardner, Mason Clark, "Russian National Guard (Rosvardia) demonstrates new capabilities in first-ever strategic exercise", Institute for the Study of War, August 17 2021, https://www.understandingwar.org/backgrounder/russian-national-guard-rosgvardia-demonstrates-new-capabilities-first-ever-strategic

Center for Strategic and International Studies, "Rosgvardiya: hurtling towards confrontation?", Sep 2020, https://www.csis.org/blogs/post-soviet-post/rosgvardiya-hurtling-towards-confrontation

Derek Lutterbeck, "Arab Uprisings, Armed Forces and Civil.Military Relations..", *Armed Forces and Society*, 39, vol 1 (Apr 2012): 28-52. https://doi.org/10.1177/0095327X12442768

Erica De Bruin, "Preventing Coups d'ètat", *The Journal of Conflict Resolution*, 62, no. 7 (August 2018): 1433-1458, https://doi.org/10.1177/0022002717692652

Grzegorz Kuczynski, "Rosvgardia receives heavy weaponry after Wagner's failed rebellion", Warsaw Institute, July 20 2023, https://warsawinstitute.org/rosgvardia-receives-heavy-weaponry-wagners-failed-rebellion/

James T. Quinlivan, "Coup-proofing: its practice and consequences in the Middle East", International Security 24, no. 2 (Fall, 1999): 131-165. http://www.jstor.org/stable/2539255

John Hardie, "Russia's National Guard to Get Tanks Following Wagner Mutiny", Long war Journal, June 29 2023, https://www.longwarjournal.org/archives/2023/06/russias-national-guard-to-get-tanks-following-wagner-mutiny.php

John Psaropoulous, "As Wagner troops marched on Moscow, Ukraine made further gains", Al Jazeera, June 28 2023, https://www.aljazeera.com/news/2023/6/28/as-wagner-troops-marched-on-moscow-ukraine-made-further-gains

Jolanta Darczewska, "Rosgvardiya: a special-purpose force". Warsaw: Point of View, Centre for Eastern Studies, 2020

Mark Galeotti, "What Turkey can learn from Russia about coup-proofing the military", War on the Rocks, Aug 2 2016, https://warontherocks.com/2016/08/what-turkey-can-learn-from-russia-about-coup-proofing-the-military/

Marvin Kalb, "Why Putin needs a praetorian guard", Brookings, May 2017, https://www.brookings.edu/articles/why-putin-needs-a-praetorian-guard/

Nickolas Bruetsch, "Я, СИЛОВИК ROSGVARDIYA: the emperor's new guards", The Security Distillery, Oct 2021, https://thesecuritydistillery.org/all-articles/-rosgvardiya-the-emperors-new-guards

Sinead Baker, "Russia's 200,000 strong national guard is getting armed with heavy weaponry, in a sign of its growing importance to Putin, UK intel says", Business Insider, Aug 8 2023, https://www.businessinsider.com/russia-national-guard-getting-heavy-weapons-defend-putin-uk-intel-2023-8?r=US&IR=T

Sky News 24, "Russia Rebellion: Wagner Group troops to be absorbed into Russian military as mercenary boss Yevgeny Prigozhin heads to Belarus", June 25 2023, https://news.sky.com/story/russia-rebellion-wagner-group-troops-to-be-absorbed-into-russian-military-as-mercenary-boss-yevgeny-prigozhin-heads-to-belarus-12909128

Timothy L. Thomas, *Kremlin Kontrol: Russia's Political-Military Reality*. Fort Leavenworth. Foreign Military Studies Office, 2017.

Zack Beauchamp, "Could Putin actually fall?", Vox, March 13 2022, https://www.vox.com/22961563/putin-russia-ukraine-coup-revolution-invasion

***Jovan Knezevic** is a 2nd year student of the Master's Degree in International Security Studies jointly offered by Scuola Superiore Universitaria Sant' Anna and University of Trento. He is Senior Researcher in Security and Defense at GEO Mondo Internazionale. His research interests include foreign and security policies, geopolitics, EU enlargement, civil-military relations, nuclear weapons and deterrence as well as international law. He is also specializing in security-related issues in Serbia, Bosnia-Herzegovina and Kosovo as well as the post-Soviet space.*

The Never-Ending Nagorno-Karabakh Conflict: Anatomy of the Armenia-Azerbaijan Strategic Dispute in the Area

Marco Rizzi

Abstract

The article provides a comprehensive analysis of the Armenia-Azerbaijan conflict, with a focus on the historical context, the Lachin Corridor, the economic disparities between the two nations, global interests and geopolitics, and potential future scenarios. The Nagorno-Karabakh region's intricate ethnic, religious, and historical complexities have fueled a longstanding dispute, leading to multiple wars. The Lachin Corridor, a vital connection between Armenia and Nagorno-Karabakh, has become a flashpoint, facing a blockade since December 2022. Economic gaps, geopolitical alliances, and global interests further complicate the situation. The article explores potential resolutions, emphasizing the critical role of international bodies in fostering peace.

Keywords:

Armenia-Azerbaijan conflict, Nagorno-Karabakh, Lachin Corridor, geopolitical interests, humanitarian crisis

I. Introduction

Armenia and Azerbaijan, neighboring countries in the Caucasus, are known for their ethnic and linguistic diversity, with a conflict centered on the Nagorno-Karabakh region. This enclave, spanning 4,400 km², lies east of Azerbaijan and hosts a predominantly Armenian population adhering to the Orthodox faith. However, the territory belongs to Azerbaijan, inhabited by Azerbaijani Turks, primarily followers of Islam. Nagorno-Karabakh declared itself an independent republic in 1991, naming itself Artsakh, a move contested by Azerbaijan, which maintains sovereignty claims over the area. In support of Artsakh, Armenia has been a steadfast ally, contributing to the complex dynamics of the conflict.

II.   Historical context

The Armenia-Azerbaijan conflict has deep historical roots stemming from the collapse of the Russian Empire and the subsequent formation of the Soviet Union in the 20th century. Joseph Stalin played a pivotal role in shaping the geopolitical landscape in 1923. During this time, he delineated the Soviet Socialist Republic of Azerbaijan and the Soviet Socialist Republic of Armenia as separate entities. Notably, Azerbaijan gained control over Nagorno-Karabakh, a region with a predominantly Armenian population. This decision by Stalin laid the foundation for a protracted conflict that persists to this day[1]

The conflict's origins are intricately tied to ethnic and territorial complexities, particularly concerning Nagorno-Karabakh, known as Artsakh in Armenian. The region holds a cultural heritage deeply intertwined with Armenian identity. However, in 1921, Stalin, who at the time was the People's Commissar for Nationalities and later became the General Secretary of the Communist Party of the USSR, made a crucial decision: he handed over the administration of Nagorno-Karabakh to the Azerbaijan Soviet Socialist Republic, further contributing to the complexities of the

---

[1] Welt Cory & Andrew S. Bowen. "Azerbaijan and Armenia: The Nagorno-Karabakh Conflict". *Congressional Research Service* R46651 (2021).

ongoing conflict, escalating ethnic pressures, and sparking tensions between Azerbaijani and Armenian communities[2].

Adding another layer of complexity is the historical persecution of the Armenian population, notably during the Armenian genocide of 1915 orchestrated by the Ottoman Empire. This tragic event resulted in the expulsion and death of approximately one million Armenians. Despite systematic denials by Turkey, the international community recognizes the historical reality of the Armenian genocide. This acknowledgment further complicates the dynamics of the Armenia-Azerbaijan conflict[3].

Armenia experienced a period of relative stability between 1918, following its liberation from the Ottoman Empire, and 1920 when it was annexed to the USSR. Similarly, Azerbaijan had a brief period of independence between 1918 and 1922 before being annexed to the USSR.

To comprehend the ongoing conflict, an examination of the geostrategic landscape of Armenia and Azerbaijan is imperative. Both countries, former members of the Russian Empire and the USSR, share a history fraught with cultural and religious disparities, akin to the relations between Spain and Morocco, North and South Korea, or China and Taiwan. Geographical proximity has not only led to political intricacies but also fostered cultural enclaves.

Throughout history, due to their geographical proximity, their populations blurred on the map, resulting in not only political but also cultural enclaves. The expansion of the Armenian Empire, Ottoman subjugation, and later annexation by the Russian Empire, with periods of possession by both powers, created numerous enclaves for both countries. The most notable are the culturally Armenian enclave of Nagorno-Karabakh and the Azeri region (not an enclave, as it is not entirely surrounded by Armenia but an exclave) of Nakhchivan, completely separated from the rest of Azerbaijan. In the waning years of the 1980s, as the Soviet Union commenced its unraveling, Armenians fervently pressed for Nagorno-Karabakh to align itself with their republic. Incensed

---

[2] Kaan Díyarbakirlioğlu, "The Nagorno-Karabakh Conflict between Azerbaijan and Armenia from the Historical Perspective". *International Journal of Social, Political and Economic Research* 7(2), 415-439 (2020).
[3] Ibid., Zaur Shiriyev and Celia Davies. "The Turkey-Armenia-Azerbaijan Triangle: The Unexpected Outcomes of the Zurich Protocols". Perceptions: *Journal of International Affairs* 18(1), 185-221 (2013).

by Armenian appeals and demonstrations, Azerbaijani pogroms erupted against Armenians in Sumgait, an industrial city distant from Nagorno-Karabakh, and in the capital, Baku, leading to ethnic cleansings on both sides. This tumultuous period eventually escalated into the First Karabakh War[4].

A truce brokered by Russia in 1994 temporarily resolved the issue for 26 years, with Armenia, the prevailing military force, asserting control over the region. During this time, Nagorno-Karabakh declared independence, albeit without formal recognition from any country, including Armenia. The international community, for the most part, favored Azerbaijan's territorial integrity claims, countered by Armenians invoking the principle of the region's national self-determination.

Over the ensuing decades, Armenians expanded their influence into other parts of Azerbaijan, displacing nearly a million Azerbaijanis from their homes. Simultaneously, hundreds of thousands of Armenians fled Azerbaijan to escape further violence. The conflict stagnated, with neither party willing to make the necessary concessions for resolution.

Azerbaijan, bolstered by oil wealth and support from loyal ally Turkey, gradually gained the upper hand. In 2020, Azerbaijani leader Ilham Aliyev, leveraging Turkish drones, Israeli weaponry, and Syrian mercenaries, initiated the Second Karabakh War. After 44 days of intense conflict, Armenian forces succumbed, and the democratically elected Armenian government, led by Nikol Pashinyan, reluctantly accepted a ceasefire mediated by Russia[5]

As Russia became engrossed in its Special Military Operation in Ukraine, Azerbaijani forces repeatedly breached the Armenian border. In December 2022, Azerbaijanis blockaded the Lachin corridor, the vital route connecting Armenia to Nagorno-Karabakh. Ostensibly an ecological protest against Armenian mining activities, Armenians perceived it as a deliberate effort to dismantle Nagorno-Karabakh and expel the last Armenian residents. The blockade, now lasting ten months, has left Nagorno-Karabakh Armenians with decreasing supplies of food and medicine.

---

[4] Kaan Díyarbakirlioğlu, "The Nagorno-Karabakh Conflict between Azerbaijan and Armenia from the Historical Perspective". *International Journal of Social, Political and Economic Research* 7(2), 415-439 (2020).

[5] Welt Cory & Andrew S. Bowen. "Azerbaijan and Armenia: The Nagorno-Karabakh Conflict". *Congressional Research Service* R46651 (2021).

Last September, Pashinyan accused Azerbaijan of increasing troop presence along the disputed Nagorno-Karabakh region and the Armenian-Azerbaijani border. Recent bombings near the border resulted in casualties on both sides, escalating tensions amid the ongoing crisis over Nagorno-Karabakh[6]

III.   Focus: Lachin Corridor

The Lachin Corridor, a slender strip of land measuring just 14 kilometers at its narrowest point, holds profound significance as the most direct connection between Armenia and Nagorno-Karabakh, nestled within the territory of Azerbaijan. Established during the Nagorno-Karabakh war, it was under the control of the Artsakh Defence Army until November 2020 when it became fully integrated into the Republic of Artsakh.

The conflicts between Armenia and Azerbaijan concerning Nagorno-Karabakh, an ethnically Armenian enclave within Azerbaijan, have been the root cause of several wars. Armenia acknowledges Nagorno-Karabakh as Artsakh, a distinct republic, leading to prolonged disputes. Despite Armenia's close ties with Russia, the region has remained a flashpoint as Azerbaijan, backed by Turkey, seeks control over it.

Since December 2022, a group of Azerbaijanis, masquerading as environmental activists, have imposed a blockade on the corridor. This action has violated existing commitments, effectively isolating the 120,000 inhabitants of Nagorno-Karabakh. The blockade stands as a stark violation of the ceasefire agreement, leaving the capital, Stepanakert, and the wider region in dire need of essential supplies.

Amid persistent border disputes over territorial integrity, Azerbaijan's insistence on establishing border control in the corridor has intensified the situation. This demand, despite global condemnation and calls for the blockade's removal, continues to exacerbate tensions, pushing the region into a deepening humanitarian crisis.

The consequences are severe—gas and electricity shortages amid harsh winters, restricted access to education, and limited medical aid. Nagorno-Karabakh faces a distressing humanitarian catastrophe. Yet, the global response remains

---

[6] Bedross Der Matossian, "Impunity, Lack of Humanitarian Intervention, and International Apathy: The Blockade of the Lachin Corridor in Historical Perspective," Genocide Studies International 15, no. 1 (2023): 7-20.

disproportionately limited, echoing past events that are all too familiar to the Armenian diaspora worldwide.

Actions and statements from Azerbaijani and Turkish leadership have raised grave concerns, signaling potential threats of genocide. The situation urgently demands attention and intervention in accordance with the UN Genocide Convention to prevent further humanitarian tragedy in the Caucasus.

This complex and ongoing conflict between Armenia and Azerbaijan over Nagorno-Karabakh's status continues to disrupt lives and threaten the region's stability. The Lachin Corridor, once a crucial lifeline connecting Armenia to Nagorno-Karabakh, has now become a flashpoint, underscoring the dire need for diplomatic solutions and international intervention to ease the suffering of the people trapped in this strife-torn region[7].

IV.   Economic gap between Armenia and Azerbaijan

The contemporary issue emerged subsequent to the dissolution of the USSR. Following this, despite the cultural identity of Nagorno-Karabakh's inhabitants aligning with Armenia, the region remained under the jurisdiction of the Soviet Socialist Republic of Azerbaijan due to strained relations between Russians and Armenians. Post the independence of both nations, the conflict erupted surrounding the region's bid for autonomy. As said, ultimately, Nagorno-Karabakh refrained from joining Armenia but established its own state, the Republic of Artsakh, albeit without international recognition. In this enclave, the prevailing language and currency are Armenian, and in practical terms, the government operates as an Armenian protectorate.

Since the fall of the USSR and the consequent Armenian-Azerbaijani conflict, both nations have undergone distinct

---

[7] Bedross Der Matossian, "Impunity, Lack of Humanitarian Intervention, and International Apathy: The Blockade of the Lachin Corridor in Historical Perspective," *Genocide Studies International* 15, no. 1 (2023): 7-20; Luis Moreno Ocampo, "Starvation as a Means of Genocide: Azerbaijan's Blockade of the Lachin Corridor Between Armenia and Nagorno-Karabakh" (2023); Wojciech Górecki, "No Special Status, No Armenians? The Prospects for Nagorno-Karabakh in a Unitary Azerbaijan" (2023); Giulia Prelz Oltramonti, "Nagorno-Karabakh: Slowly but Surely, Baku Is Weaponising the Green Movement to Cut Off the Region's Supplies" (2023).

trajectories. While corruption remains a prevalent issue, and neither country is categorized as a developed state, Azerbaijan has outpaced Armenia in economic terms. With a population exceeding three times that of Armenia, Azerbaijan boasts a per capita GDP of €7,300, surpassing Armenia's €6,100. Moreover, Azerbaijan exhibits a significantly lower unemployment rate, constituting half of that in Armenia. Notably, Azerbaijan maintains a debt-to-GDP ratio of 20%, while Armenia's stands at 60%. The discernible economic gap is evident from Azerbaijan's national GDP of €74.645 billion compared to Armenia's €18.451 billion.

Furthermore, Azerbaijan demonstrates a positive trade balance exceeding €8.5 billion, while Armenia contends with a negative balance close to €2 billion. Despite grappling with corruption issues, Azerbaijan has exhibited more adept management of its economic affairs in contrast to Armenia.

This economic discrepancy has led to a role reversal, with Azerbaijan now wielding a more developed economy, a fortified state, and a more formidable military force than its counterpart. Motivated by a desire to divert attention from internal corruption, Azerbaijan is eager to settle historical scores, transforming the conflict into not just a matter of national pride but a strategic maneuver in Azerbaijan's political landscape.

Significantly, owing to its territorial exclave, Azerbaijan not only seeks to reclaim Nagorno-Karabakh but also intends to secure a corridor from Armenian territory connecting its separated regions. This poses a direct challenge to Armenia's sovereignty, previously limited to claims over the Republic of Artsakh, a region officially independent from Armenia. Recognizing its inferiority to Azerbaijan, Armenia has used this pretext to refrain from defending Nagorno-Karabakh, leading to internal unrest, particularly among nationalist factions[8].

---

[8] Laurence Broers, Armenia and Azerbaijan: Anatomy of a Rivalry, Edinburgh *University Press, 2019*; Chester English, "Armenia: Overcoming Economic and Geopolitical Obstacles" (2023); Gubad Ibadoghlu and Ibrahim Niftiyev, "An Assessment of the Thirty Year Post-Soviet Transition Quality in Azerbaijan from an Economic and Social Liberalization Perspective," *Journal of Life Economics* 9, no. 3 (2022): 129-146; Emre Çitak, "Azerbaijan in the 21st Century: An Assessment in the Context of Main Determinants of Domestic and Foreign Policies," *The Changing Perspectives and 'New' Geopolitics of the Caucasus in the 21st Century* 38, no. 1 (2021): 19; Oana-Ramona Socoliuc and Liviu-George Maha, "The Economic

V.   Global interests and geopolitics around the conflict

When examining the geopolitical landscape in this context, one might expect a straightforward division where Muslim-majority nations and Russia align with Azerbaijan, while the Western bloc supports Armenia. However, the reality is far more convoluted. Azerbaijan, deeply rooted in its Ottoman heritage, forges a resilient partnership with Turkey. Consequently, if NATO member Turkey throws its weight behind Azerbaijan, historical adversaries like Russia and Iran find themselves siding with Armenia. This intricate web of alignments, influenced by historical intricacies, sees Russia, once the overseer of Nagorno-Karabakh under Azerbaijani control due to historical animosity with Armenians, now safeguarding Armenian interests. Iran, often associated with a regime of radical Islamic governance, paradoxically allies with the Christian nation, introducing an unexpected twist. This complex network of affiliations takes an unforeseen turn as Israel, contrary to expectations, aligns itself with the Muslim side, diverging from its position in the Gaza Strip.

Geopolitics emerges prominently in the Armenian-Azerbaijani conflict. Noticeably absent from active engagement are the United States and the European Union, both proceeding cautiously. The U.S., instead of committing unequivocally, adopts a strategic stance of nonalignment, acknowledging that abstaining from picking sides might prove the most prudent course in certain circumstances. The United States closely monitors unfolding events, seemingly finding advantage in a prolonged conflict that undermines the image of its adversary, Russia. The prolonged strife particularly harms Russia's standing, given the membership of both Armenia and Azerbaijan in the Commonwealth of Independent States, an organization striving for collaboration among former USSR members in defense, economy, and security. While these member states are expected to follow Russia's lead, the reality is nuanced. Notably, countries like Latvia, Lithuania, Estonia, Georgia, Ukraine, and Turkmenistan either refrained from joining or departed from the CIS. A conflict between two CIS

Dynamics of the Eastern Partnership Countries: Between Development Gaps and Internal Fragilities," in *Resilience and the EU's Eastern Neighbourhood Countries: From Theoretical Concepts to a Normative Agenda* (2019): 89-135.

members, Armenia and Azerbaijan, erodes Russia's authority, offering a strategic opportunity for the U.S. to leverage[9].

Adding depth to the geopolitical puzzle is Armenia's affiliation with the Collective Security Treaty Organization (CSTO), often likened to Russia's counterpart to NATO. Conversely, Azerbaijan does not share this alliance. The CSTO mandates immediate Russian mobilization for Armenia's defense in the face of an external threat. The absence of rapid support further tarnishes Russia's already diminished image. This noticeable inaction might prompt other nations to reconsider the perceived efficacy of Russian "protection".

In the context of the European Union's interests, the ongoing Armenia-Azerbaijan conflict holds significance, although seemingly from the EU as a whole. Despite involving two relatively small, distant, and underdeveloped countries locked in a territorial dispute around the Caspian Sea, the ramifications extend far beyond their borders.

The global landscape is currently grappling with an inflation crisis driven by multiple factors, notably the surge in energy prices due to the conflict in Ukraine and strained relations with Russia. While both the U.S. and Russia possess substantial oil reserves, Europe finds itself disproportionately affected, particularly evident during OPEC meetings. Europe's lack of oil production coupled with a significant dependence on Russia exacerbates the situation.

The war in Ukraine further impacts gas prices, with the U.S. and Russia experiencing relatively minimal effects compared to Europe. Sanctions on Russia have led to Europe relying on liquefied gas trade, significantly inflating prices. This disparity is stark, with U.S. citizens paying substantially less than their European counterparts for gas, highlighting a high price difference.

Not surprisingly, the Armenia-Azerbaijan conflict intertwines with this scenario. Despite Azerbaijan's status as a developing country, its emergence as a regional power relies heavily on oil and gas. Strategically, Azerbaijan finds itself without major power backing for its claims, presenting an opportunity for

---

[9] Harun Semercioğlu, "The New Balance of Power in the Southern Caucasus in the Context of the Nagorno-Karabakh Conflict in 2020," *R&S-Research Studies Anatolia Journal* 4, no. 1 (2021): 49-60; Amir Jan et al., "The Geo-Political Implications of the Nagorno-Karabakh Conflict," *Journal of Critical Reviews* 8, no. 2 (2021); Botakoz Kazbek, "Existing Powers and Alliances Before the 2020 War in Nagorny Karabakh" (2021).

Europe. The operational Southern Gas Corridor, established in collaboration with European nations, facilitates the flow of natural gas from Azerbaijan to Europe. This strategic move aims to reduce Europe's reliance on Russian gas, a stance solidified even before the Ukrainian crisis.

Europe's diminishing gas demand, driven by consumption reduction policies, energy efficiency measures, and renewable energy promotion, indicates a downward trend in dependence on external resources. However, Azerbaijan's potential to provide stable gas supply at a reasonable price aligns with Europe's aim to reduce reliance on strategic resources it cannot internally produce.

Strategically, Europe's interests diverge from those of the U.S. While supporting Azerbaijan to ensure a steady flow of resources is vital for Europe's energy security, a cautious approach is necessary. The aim is to pacify the region to guarantee the uninterrupted flow of crucial resources for Europe. This contrasts with potential ambitions of Azerbaijan to not only secure Nagorno-Karabakh but also to retain control over the gas corridor[10].

Recent developments indicate Armenia's shifting alliances, realizing the limitations of Russian protection. Armenia's engagements with Western nations and seeking independence from Russian influence underscore the evolving dynamics in the region.

As Europe navigates its energy security strategy, the Armenia-Azerbaijan conflict takes on a new significance, shaping alliances and influencing resource dynamics in the region, which could have lasting implications for Europe's energy independence and geopolitical standing.

---

[10] Elmar Mustafayev, "EU Values and Interests in the Resolution of Nagorno-Karabakh Conflict," *Insight Turkey* 23, no. 2 (2021): 65-81; Stefan Meister and Laure Delcour, "The Armenia-Azerbaijan Conflict: What Role Now for the EU in the South Caucasus after Nagorno-Karabakh?" (2023): 7; G. R. Basharov, F. S. Shedko, D. P. Okolota, A. L. Kotova, and A. A. Volkova, "Ecological Dimension of Conflict in Nagorno-Karabakh," in *E3S Web of Conferences* 311 (2021); Esmira Jafarova, "The Role of the United States in the Armenia–Azerbaijan Conflict," in *The Nagorno-Karabakh Conflict* (Routledge, 2022), 321-340; Welt Cory & Andrew S. Bowen. "Azerbaijan and Armenia: The Nagorno-Karabakh Conflict." *Congressional Research Service* R46651 (2021).

VI. **Looking ahead: analysis of future scenarios, further developments, and challenges in the resolution of the conflict**

The ongoing conflict between Armenia and Azerbaijan, deeply rooted in history, politics, and military tensions, continues to pose a formidable challenge. Despite multiple international efforts to broker peace, including recent initiatives by the European Union and the efforts of the Council of Europe, finding a resolution remains elusive. The trajectory of this complex situation hinges on several critical factors:

The most desirable pathway to resolution involves diplomatic negotiations between the conflicting parties or facilitated by impartial international bodies like the European Union. Russia's involvement, so far, hasn't yielded significant progress. For a meaningful breakthrough, both sides must demonstrate unwavering commitment, and the engagement of neutral entities such as the Organization for Security and Cooperation in Europe (OSCE) could prove crucial.

A second potential solution involves granting Nagorno-Karabakh substantial autonomy within Azerbaijan while safeguarding the rights of its Armenian population. This proposition, once considered within Azerbaijan, lost traction when fears of repression drove most Armenians to leave the region, essentially sidelining the prospect of autonomy.

A complex but deliberated third option revolves around a territorial swap that mirrors present ethnic demographics. This maneuver aims to align territorial boundaries with the distribution of Armenian and Azerbaijani populations, seeking to establish coherence between ethnicity and territory.

The last option possible preludes a risk of escalation. Despite being the least desirable scenario, there's a looming concern in Baku about potentially reigniting conflict. Speculation suggests intentions to establish a connection between the Nakhichevan enclave and the rest of Azerbaijan through the Zangezur corridor. However, this would violate Armenia's recognized borders and could trigger unforeseeable global responses, including Iran's warning of considering it a declaration of war, pledging support for Armenia[11].

---

[11] Wojciech Górecki, "No Special Status, No Armenians? The Prospects for Nagorno-Karabakh in a Unitary Azerbaijan" (2023); Vladimir M. Morozov, "The Network Diplomacy Model in the Context of Nagorno-Karabakh: Prospects for Conflict Resolution," in

Moreover, discussions also center on the plight of Christian communities in the Middle East. Long subjected to persecution, the annexation of Nagorno-Karabakh forced over 120,000 Christians to flee lands they inhabited for centuries, adding to the historical expulsion of communities in Armenia, Syria, Iraq, and Anatolia.

Addressing the Armenia-Azerbaijan conflict necessitates sincere commitment from both parties and robust international mediation, with the European Union emerging as a key player. This underscores the EU's pivotal role in countering Moscow's influence, which has proven unreliable and destabilizing in various regions[12].

A resolution in this region extends far beyond the interests of Armenia and Azerbaijan. It holds significant implications for stability in the Caucasus and, by extension, Europe. Achieving a lasting peace is imperative to halt prolonged suffering and cultivate prosperity in the region. The complexities involved demand concerted efforts and a readiness to engage in dialogue and compromise from all stakeholders involved.

Network Diplomacy: Contributing to Peace in the 21st Century (Singapore: Springer Nature Singapore, 2022), 149-165; Davor Boban and Iva Blažević, "The Failure of The Nagorno-Karabakh Conflict Resolution: Shortcomings of Facilitative Mediation or an Unsuitable Mediator?," *Politička misao: časopis za politologiju* 60, no. 2 (2023): 69-92; Benyamin Poghosyan, "Perspectives of Nagorno Karabakh Conflict Settlement Process after the September 2022," *National Interest* 2, no. 10 (2022): 26-36.

[12] Azad Garibov, "OSCE and Conflict Resolution in the Post-Soviet Area: The Case of the Armenia-Azerbaijan Nagorno-Karabakh Conflict," *Caucasus International* 5, no. 2 (2015): 75-90; Valeri Modebadze, "The Escalation of Conflict Between Armenians and Azerbaijanis and the Problems of Peaceful Resolution of the Nagorno-Karabakh War," *Journal of Liberty and International Affairs* 6, no. 3 (2021): 102-110; Giulia Prelz Oltramonti, "Nagorno-Karabakh: Slowly but Surely, Baku Is Weaponising the Green Movement to Cut Off the Region's Supplies" (2023).

Bibliography

Amir Jan et al., "The Geo-Political Implications of the Nagorno-Karabakh Conflict," Journal of Critical Reviews 8, no. 2 (2021).

Azad Garibov, "OSCE and Conflict Resolution in the Post-Soviet Area: The Case of the Armenia-Azerbaijan Nagorno-Karabakh Conflict," Caucasus International 5, no. 2 (2015): 75-90.

Bedross Der Matossian, "Impunity, Lack of Humanitarian Intervention, and International Apathy: The Blockade of the Lachin Corridor in Historical Perspective," Genocide Studies International 15, no. 1 (2023): 7-20.

Benyamin Poghosyan, "Perspectives of Nagorno Karabakh Conflict Settlement Process after the September 2022," *National Interest* 2, no. 10 (2022): 26-36.

Botakoz Kazbek, "Existing Powers and Alliances Before the 2020 War in Nagorny Karabakh" (2021).

Chester English, "Armenia: Overcoming Economic and Geopolitical Obstacles" (2023).

Davor Boban and Iva Blažević, "The Failure of The Nagorno-Karabakh Conflict Resolution: Shortcomings of Facilitative Mediation or an Unsuitable Mediator?," *Politička misao: časopis za politologiju* 60, no. 2 (2023): 69-92.

Elmar Mustafayev, "EU Values and Interests in the Resolution of Nagorno-Karabakh Conflict," Insight Turkey 23, no. 2 (2021): 65-81.

Emre Çitak, "Azerbaijan in the 21st Century: An Assessment in the Context of Main Determinants of Domestic and Foreign Policies," The Changing Perspectives and 'New' Geopolitics of the Caucasus in the 21st Century 38, no. 1 (2021): 19.

Esmira Jafarova, "The Role of the United States in the Armenia–Azerbaijan Conflict," in The Nagorno-Karabakh Conflict (Routledge, 2022), 321-340.

Giulia Prelz Oltramonti, "Nagorno-Karabakh: Slowly but Surely, Baku Is Weaponising the Green Movement to Cut Off the Region's Supplies" (2023).

G. R. Basharov, F. S. Shedko, D. P. Okolota, A. L. Kotova, and A. A. Volkova, "Ecological Dimension of Conflict in Nagorno-Karabakh," in E3S Web of Conferences 311 (2021).

Gubad Ibadoghlu and Ibrahim Niftiyev, "An Assessment of the Thirty Year Post-Soviet Transition Quality in Azerbaijan from an Economic and Social Liberalization Perspective," Journal of Life Economics 9, no. 3 (2022): 129-146.

Harun Semercioğlu, "The New Balance of Power in the Southern Caucasus in the Context of the Nagorno-Karabakh Conflict in 2020," R&S-Research Studies Anatolia Journal 4, no. 1 (2021): 49-60.

Kaan Díyarbakirlioğlu, "The Nagorno-Karabakh Conflict between Azerbaijan and Armenia from the Historical Perspective," *International Journal of Social, Political and Economic Research* 7, no. 2 (2020): 415-439.

Laurence Broers, Armenia and Azerbaijan: Anatomy of a Rivalry (Edinburgh University Press, 2019).

Luis Moreno Ocampo, "Starvation as a Means of Genocide: Azerbaijan's Blockade of the Lachin Corridor Between Armenia and Nagorno-Karabakh" (2023).

Oana-Ramona Socoliuc and Liviu-George Maha, "The Economic Dynamics of the Eastern Partnership Countries: Between Development Gaps and Internal Fragilities," in Resilience and the EU's Eastern Neighbourhood Countries: From Theoretical Concepts to a Normative Agenda (2019): 89-135.

Stefan Meister and Laure Delcour, "The Armenia-Azerbaijan Conflict: What Role Now for the EU in the South Caucasus after Nagorno-Karabakh?" (2023): 7.

Valeri Modebadze, "The Escalation of Conflict Between Armenians and Azerbaijanis and the Problems of Peaceful

Resolution of the Nagorno-Karabakh War," Journal of Liberty and International Affairs 6, no. 3 (2021): 102-110.

Vladimir M. Morozov, "The Network Diplomacy Model in the Context of Nagorno-Karabakh: Prospects for Conflict Resolution," in *Network Diplomacy: Contributing to Peace in the 21st Century* (Singapore: Springer Nature Singapore, 2022), 149-165.

Welt, Cory, and Andrew S. Bowen. "Azerbaijan and Armenia: The Nagorno-Karabakh Conflict." Congressional Research Service R46651 (2021).

Wojciech Górecki, "No Special Status, No Armenians? The Prospects for Nagorno-Karabakh in a Unitary Azerbaijan" (2023).

Zaur Shiriyev and Celia Davies, "The Turkey-Armenia-Azerbaijan Triangle: The Unexpected Outcomes of the Zurich Protocols," Perceptions: Journal of International Affairs 18, no. 1 (2013): 185-221.

Marco Rizzi was born in Milan, Italy in 2000. He completed his undergraduate studies in 'International Relations and Global Affairs' at Università Cattolica del Sacro Cuore in June 2022. His thesis explored the Spitzenkandidaten system and its role within the European Union. Intrigued by Europe's global influence, he pursued a Master's in 'European Affairs' at the University of Lund, Sweden. Serving as Head of Lecture at the Association of Foreign Affairs in Lund, Marco encourages discussions on international issues. Additionally, he writes for The Perspective and is a Senior Researcher to Mondo Internazionale, both media outlet platforms specializing in global foreign policy and current events. Since last September, Marco has been a Trainee at the EU Delegation to the Council of Europe in Strasbourg. He is fluent in Italian, English, French, and Spanish.

Asia-Pacific

Myanmar's Gender-Based Violence and Patriarchal Culture: Impacts on Ethnic Cleansing and the Importance of a Gendered Approach to Peacebuilding

Ilenia Bruseghello, Mariavittoria Maggi, and Giorgia Piovesan

Abstract

This paper provides a comprehensive overview of gender-based violence (GBV) in Myanmar, with a focus on the patriarchal structure dominating the country's culture and particularly the 'inborn holiness' (*hpon*) attributed to men and its effect on the country's development and societal well-being. The intrinsic instability of the country, due to ethnic conflicts and gender repressive norms, results in cases of brutal ethnic cleansing consisting of various forms of GBV committed by the Myanmar military and security forces, such as sexual assault, mutilation of reproductive organs, and sexual humiliation. Analysing the case of the Rohingya community, this paper aims at shedding light on the link between the patriarchal and cultural *hpon* and the systematic impunity of the military's use of GBV, further allowing its employment as a means of genocidal strategy. Finally, drawing on the 2015-2016 ceasefire negotiations signed between the government and the paramilitary groups, this paper argues that a lack of consideration towards gender issues contributed to their consequent failure. Peace-building efforts should rely on an alternative gendered approach at the societal level to be effective. Its application in the context of the present-day conflict can prove beneficial in building long-lasting political stability.

Keywords: gender-based violence (GBV), Myanmar, patriarchal society, ethnic conflicts, ethnic cleansing, Rohingya, military, genocidal strategy, gender issues, peacebuilding, *hpon*

I.   Introduction

Myanmar's societal structure, rooted in religious beliefs attributing men a higher status, paves the way for social inequalities and women's marginalisation from civic participation. This results in women's exclusion from decision-making and political processes, particularly those concerning military and security matters such as ceasefire negotiations. This practice leads to the absence of a gender perspective, leaving women in a position of vulnerability and insecurity. Women's exclusion is further aggravated by the fact that they are the main victims of gender-based violence (GBV), which is particularly employed as a war tool to pursue ethnic cleansing to target the Rohingya community. In this paper, we argue that a gender-sensitive approach to peace negotiations would have increased peace sustainability and reduced conflict-related sexual violence and women's vulnerability.

II.   Patriarchal social structure and religious norms: roots of gender-based violence

Myanmar's cultural fabric is intricately woven with religious and patriarchal tenets, a prevailing force that significantly perpetuates gender inequality and contributes to the alarming prevalence of violence against women.[1] Gender-based violence (GBV) encompasses various forms of violence or threats targeting individuals based on their sex, gender identity, or sexual orientation: it can include physical, psychological, sexual, verbal, and economic abuse, and it is deeply rooted in gender inequalities and power imbalances, impacting women and girls in particular.[2]

Religion still yields strong influence over beliefs and practices related to human conduct, inculcating male ascendancy and relegating women to subordinate positions, serving as a potent

---

[1] Ardiff Helena, "Sexual and Gender-Based Violence in Myanmar and the Gendered Impact of Its Ethnic Conflicts." Office of the United Nations High Commissioner for Human Rights, August 22, 2019.

[2] Davies Sara E. and Jacqui True "The Politics of Counting and Reporting Conflict-Related Sexual and Gender-Based Violence: The Case of Myanmar." *International Feminist Journal of Politics 19*, no. 1 (2017): 7

mechanism in the perpetuation of violence against women. In Theravada Buddhist societies, including Myanmar, the concept of *hpon*, has been used to justify the perceived higher authority and status of men in religious matters. *Hpon* is often understood as a spiritual merit or virtue that is believed to accumulate through one's actions and intentions in previous lives.[3] It is believed to have an impact on one's current social position, including one's gender. According to this belief system, men are seen as having accumulated higher *hpon* in previous lives, which grants them a higher religious status and authority over their women in the present life: female participation in decision-making in the political, administrative, and economic spheres is indeed very limited.[4]

These beliefs find no basis in religious texts, however, and by attributing discriminatory practices to religion, their origins in patriarchal structures are obscured, granting them a false sense of legitimacy.[5] Consequently, even as societal circumstances evolve, the stigmatization of gender inequality persists and manifests in new forms.

III.   Gender blindness in the 2015 ceasefire agreement

On October 15th, 2015, Myanmar's government and eight out of the sixteen major ethnic armed groups engaged in the conflict signed the Nationwide Ceasefire Agreement (NCA). Ceasefires are characterised by their aim to suspend violence and fighting so that more comprehensive and permanent peace negotiations may take place.[6] The marginalisation of women is a common aspect of ceasefire negotiations, justified by the notion that these agreements are military processes necessitating technical knowledge of military forces.[7]

---

[3] Nwe, Than Tha, "Gendered spaces: Women in Burmese society" *Transfor- mations* (2003): 9

[4] Unknown,"UNHEARD VOICES Qualitative Research on Conflict-Related Sexual Violence in Myanmar (2016-2021)", United Nations Office of the Special Representative of the Secretary-General on Sexual Violence in Conflict , June 19, 2022.

[5] Tun Thein Pansy, "Gender Equality and Cultural Norms in Myanmar" *International Conference on Burma/Myanmar Studies: Burma/Myanmar in Transition: Connectivity, Changes and Challenges*: (July 2015).

[6] Barsa, Michelle et al., "Inclusive Ceasefires: Women, gender, and a sustainable end to violence," *Inclusive Security* (2016): 3.

Myanmar's ceasefire negotiations, which spanned over 18 months, did not account for women's participation, and their involvement was mostly limited to logistical roles such as notetaking, transportation, and cooking, rather than a meaningful contribution to the formal decision-making processes. A total of five women were present amongst the overall 94 individuals composing the negotiation bodies, and only four of the 61 signatories were women.[8]

The result of this underrepresentation is an agreement that lacks a gendered perspective, where the vagueness of the language used does not forbid indirect discrimination based on gender, and where "citizens" are referenced as the only individuals protected by the agreement, excluding stateless persons such as the Rohingya. Moreover, sexual and gender-based violence is not an explicit violation of the agreement, therefore no mechanism is implemented to monitor it.[9]

IV.   Gender-based violence: a tool of ethnic cleansing against the Rohingyas

The perpetual ethnic conflicts and political instability that have beleaguered Myanmar have substantially exacerbated the prevalence of GBV. These protracted conflicts engender forced displacement, sexual violence, and, most harrowingly, ruthless acts of ethnic cleansing.[10] The women and girls from the Rohingya community, a Muslim ethnic minority originally from Rakhine state, have been the primary victims of gender-based violence.

On August 26th, 2017, the Myanmar military launched the "clearance operation," a massive counter-insurgency campaign against the rebel group Arakan Rohingya Salvation Army (ARSA), which ultimately led to indiscriminate and widespread violence against the Rohingya community. In the same year, the UN Independent International Fact-Finding

---

[7] Robert Forster and Christine Bell, "Gender Mainstreaming in Ceasefires: Comparative Data and Examples," (New, 2019), 12; Barsa et al. (2016), p. 50.

[8] Barsa et al. (2016), p. 25, 26.

[9] *Ivi, p. 28.*

[10] Alam, Mayesha, and Jean Wood, Elisabeth. "Ideology and the Implicit Authorization of Violence as Policy: The Myanmar Military's Conflict-Related Sexual Violence against the Rohingya." *Journal of Global Security Studies 7*, no. 2 (2022): 3

Mission on Myanmar (IIFFMM) reported that "sexual and gender-based violence had been committed on a massive scale" against the Rohingyas in twenty-seven localities in the Northern Rakhine State.[11]

In post-coup Myanmar, the military's brutal crackdown and lawlessness have led to a surge in sexual violence as GBV has been used as a weapon in the Rohingya genocide, accompanied by other strategies such as land confiscation and forced eviction.[12] The repertoire of violence suffered by Rohingya civilians includes various forms of GBV aimed at humiliating the community, especially undermining their reproductive capacity[13], with men and women targeted separately. Men were mostly tortured, mutilated, castrated, abused, and subjected to penis mutilation and anal rape before their execution. Women suffered public and gang rape, sexualised torture during massacres, genital mutilation, sexual assault, forced witnessing, and other forms of violence. Analysing the brutal practices, it is possible to note a systemic use of GBV for ethnic cleansing: male genital mutilation and the beating of pregnant women not only aim at the identity humiliation but also undermine its reproductive capacity and are employed as a deliberate tactic for acts of genocide. By subjecting women to such violence, the aim is also to instil fear and terror within the target group, compelling them to flee the territory. The militarised masculinity and patriarchal culture allowed for the widespread use of rape as a war tool and gang rape as a social cohesion practice, which was not just tolerated, but perpetrated by soldiers as well as the Command, creating a fertile terrain for impunity[14].

### V.	Women's inclusion: enhancing peace, equality, and sustainability

The final text of the NCA called for the inclusion of a "reasonable number/ratio of women representatives in the political dialogue process," however no exact number or ratio

---

[11] Alam, M., and Jean Wood, E. (2022), p. 2; IIFFMM (2019,4); US Department of State (2018, 8-15).

[12] Anwary, Afroza. "Sexual violence against women as a weapon of Rohingya genocide in Myanmar." *The International Journal of Human Rights 26*, no. 3 (2022): 412.

[13] Alam, Mayesha, and Elisabeth Jean Wood. (2022). p. 2.

[14] *Ivi,* pp. 3 – 8, 13.

had been fixed, and an agreement of around 30 percent was implicitly reached.[15] Women's participation quotas are favoured, as it is believed that women's direct involvement in the negotiations would produce stronger provisions concerning the involvement of male allies. The inclusion of women in monitoring efforts also increases reporting of gender-based violations, particularly sexual violence.[16]

The exclusion of gendered perspectives created a socio-political context perpetuating women's insecurity: women are responsible for extensive (unpaid) care work, and the absence of social provisions among reform measures directly contributes to their exclusion from arising socio-economic opportunities.[17] Consequently, gendered power dynamics are reinforced, exacerbating disparities and leaving women more vulnerable to poverty and exploitation. Given that women comprise more than half of Myanmar's population since the early 2000s,[18] the majority of individuals living in the country suffer from this heightened vulnerability.

Increased suffering for most of the population is not the sole reason to include gendered perspectives in ceasefire processes, as research has shown that "[w]omen have a positive impact on the success and sustainability of comprehensive peace negotiations."[19] Potential benefits of gender representation in ceasefire negotiations include increased societal support and legitimization, the perception of women as trustworthy intermediaries, and an improved understanding of the threat environment.[20] These benefits ultimately lead to a higher likelihood of reaching an agreement during negotiations, increased implementation rates, and reduced risk of relapse into conflict.[21] Women's direct involvement also ensures

---

[15] Barsa et al. (2016). p. 29.

[16] *Ivi,* pp. 32, 40, 42.

[17] Hedström, "On violence, the everyday, and social reproduction: Agnes and Myanmar's transition," 380; Jenny Hedström and Elisabeth Olivius, "Insecurity, Dispossession, Depletion: Women's Experiences of Post-War Development in Myanmar," *The European Journal of Development Research* 32, no. 2 (2020/04/01 2020): 381.

[18] The World Bank, "Population, female (% of total population) - Myanmar," (The World Bank, 2023).

[19] Barsa et al. (2016). p. 49.

[20] *Ivi,* p. 5-8.

greater attention is paid to gender equality from the early stages of peace processes and throughout the subsequent transition.[22] If negotiations will take place in the future to address the ongoing tensions, it is vital to learn from the past and ensure women's involvement, as it would increase the sustainability and comprehensiveness of the peace process.

VI.   Conclusion

The ubiquitous nature of patriarchal culture and its defining impact on religious practices in Myanmar have forged an environment where the voices of women remain stifled and their representation marginalized. The roots of gender-based discrimination are further compounded during times of internal strife and the aftermath of conflicts, wherein the authority conferred to men becomes an odious pretext for perpetrating heinous acts of rape, violence, and the abhorrent slaughter of Rohingya women and girls. The insidious cloak of impunity not only stems from the deeply entrenched male hierarchy but is also woven into the very Myanmar government policy to exterminate the vulnerable Rohingya ethnic group. The exclusion of women in peace processes and ceasefires perpetuates gendered insecurity; to address ongoing tensions and future negotiations, it is crucial to break this vicious circle and ensure women's involvement.

---

[21] Jacqueline H. R. Demeritt, Angela D. Nichols, and Eliza G. Kelly, "Female Participation and Civil War Relapse," *Civil Wars* 16, no. 3 (2014/07/03 2014): 362.
[22] Barsa et al. (2016). p. 49.

Bibliography:

Alam, Mayesha, and Elisabeth Jean Wood. "Ideology and the Implicit Authorization of Violence as Policy: The Myanmar Military's Conflict-Related Sexual Violence against the Rohingya." *Journal of Global Security Studies 7*, no. 2 (2022)

Anwary, Afroza. "Sexual violence against women as a weapon of Rohingya genocide in Myanmar." *The International Journal of Human Rights 26*, no. 3 (2022): 400-419.
Barsa, Michelle, Olivia Holt-Ivry, Allison Muehlenbeck, Kelly Case, Tiffany Easthom, Marie O'Reilly, and Julia Palmiano Federer. "Inclusive Ceasefires: Women, Gender, and a Sustainable End to Violence." *Inclusive Security* (2016)

Demeritt, Jacqueline H. R., Angela D. Nichols, and Eliza G. Kelly. "Female Participation and Civil War Relapse." *Civil Wars 16*, no. 3 (2014): 346-368.

Forster, Robert, and Christine Bell. "Gender Mainstreaming in Ceasefires: Comparative Data and Examples." *New* (2019)

Hedström, Jenny. "On violence, the everyday, and social reproduction: Agnes and Myanmar's transition." *Peacebuilding 9*, no. 4 (2021): 371-386.

Hedström, Jenny, and Elisabeth Olivius. "Insecurity, Dispossession, Depletion: Women's Experiences of Post-War Development in Myanmar." *The European Journal of Development Research 32*, no. 2 (2020): 379-403.

Miedema, S. S., and A. T. Kyaw. "Women's intergenerational intimate partner violence and household child abuse in Burma (Myanmar)." *SSM Popul Health 17* (2022)

Priddy, Grace, Zoe Doman, Emily Berry, and Saleh Ahmed. "Gender-based violence in a complex humanitarian context: Unpacking the human sufferings among stateless Rohingya women." *Ethnicities 22*, no. 2 (2022): 215-232.

The World Bank. "Population, Female (% of Total Population) - Myanmar." The World Bank, 2023.

Tun Thein, Pansy. "Gender Equality and Cultural Norms in Myanmar." *International Conference on Burma/Myanmar Studies: Burma/Myanmar in Transition: Connectivity, Changes and Challenges*, July 2015.

United Nations (UNHRC). "Sexual and gender-based violence in Myanmar and the gendered impact of its ethnic conflicts." Geneva: UN, 2019.

"UNHEARD VOICES Qualitative Research on Conflict-Related Sexual Violence in Myanmar (2016-2021)." United Nations Office of the Special Representative of the Secretary-General on Sexual Violence in Conflict, June 19, 2022.

__Ilenia Bruseghello__ is a former cadet of the Italian Navy with three years of experience in the military field. She holds a Bachelor's Degree in Political Science and International Relations from Sapienza University of Rome (IT) and she is currently pursuing an International Master's Degree in Security, Intelligence and Strategic Studies. She is a Nuclear Risk Fellow at ERA Cambridge (UK), where she conducts cutting-edge research on unmanned systems and the challenges posed by nuclear risk mitigation. She is also a NATO Public Diplomacy Division Grantee with experience in project management and policy development. Her main areas of interest include emerging technologies, space security, arms control, disarmament, and non-proliferation.

__Mariavittoria Maggi__ holds a Bachelor's Degree in Economics and Business Management and is now pursuing an International Master's in Security Intelligence and Strategic Studies (IMSISS). Her research is dedicated to migration governance and the EU foreign and security policy, including the European Neighbourhood Policy and civilian CSDP missions in North Africa and the Mediterranean. As a dedicated Amnesty International activist, she passionately advocates for the upholding of human rights globally.

__Giorgia Piovesan__ obtained a Bachelor's degree in Political Science and International Relations, from Università degli Studi di Roma Tre in Italy. Following her graduation, she worked as a Cyber Security Analyst for Emerging Technologies for Deloitte, where she acquired valuable technical skills. However, her passion for international security, particularly in the East Asian region, as well as the Middle East and North Africa, prompted her to join the International Master in Security, Intelligence and Strategic Studies. Giorgia plans to focus on Strategic and War Studies in her pursuit of advanced education.

North Korea: Between Human Rights and Denuclearization

Giulia Rossi

"The only reason that we cannot claim that North Korea is the worst human rights disaster in the world today is because we are not allowed to see the extent of it"

Victor Cha[1]

Abstract

According to Human Rights Watch, North Korea has ratified six human rights treaties, even though there is no proof that these have been effectively implemented. Numerous studies have focused on the violations perpetrated by the authoritarian government and the sanctions imposed on the country by the international community. However, nearly none of them have analyzed the possibility of a change in the country's approach towards human rights. Considering North Korea as capable of change in its human rights approach is an important milestone also for a denuclearization dialogue. Indeed, this paper considers an improvement in the regime's human rights approach, as a precondition for every denuclearization attempt.

This paper, presuming that North Korea is capable of change, will analyse a range of subversive strategies that could be used to develop a dissident community inside North Korea. The paper will then argue that a more direct approach, based on the actions of the oppressed population, will undermine the regime and lead to the establishment of a more human rights-oriented government. In doing so, the role of the International Community and the question of the denuclearization of the Peninsula will be also taken into consideration, both of which are seen as complementary to the Human Rights situation.

Keywords: North Korea, change, human rights, denuclearization, bottom-up

---

[1] Victor Cha, *The Impossible State. North Korea Past and Future* (New York, NY: Ecco, 2012), 166.

I.   Introduction

For the past several years, North Korea has faced international criticism for its human rights abuses and, according to Freedom House, it ranks among the least free societies in the world.[2] However, the Democratic People's Republic of Korea (DPRK) is a party to numerous human rights treaties, such as the Convention on the Elimination of All Forms of Discrimination against Women of 1979.[3] In this paper I will analyze the North Korean case through the lens of change, considering that, with the latter form of engagement, North Korea is capable of changing its human rights situation. In the first part of this article, I will present the human rights situation existing inside the country. In the second part, I will analyse the meaning of change and how this could be applied to the DPRK. Lastly, I will investigate how human rights and denuclearization are deeply interconnected in the case of North Korea.

II.   Human Rights Situation in North Korea

The human rights portrayal of North Korea "as an Orwellian society controlled by a regime unwilling and unable to [...provide for...] its people, is largely informed by interviews with refugees, defectors, or escaped prisoners, and satellite photos of prisons."[4] To confirm this statement it has to be taken into account the chronic food shortage crisis that North Korea has suffered over the past two decades; indeed, according to the US Congress, more than 2 million people died from famine and food aids were diverted only to the elitè and the military.

Human Rights violations, as reported by various defectors, include cases of abduction, human trafficking, systematic starvation and all the gross human rights abuses perpetrated by the North Korean authorities within the detention and correctional facilities of the country. [5]According to Grace M. Kang "prisoners are arbitrarily detained and forcibly transferred to labor camps without adequate due process;

---

[2] Freedom House, "Freedom in the world 2012."

[3] Kondoch, *The responsibility to protect and Northeast Asia*, 438.

[4] Paul Liem, "Peace as a North Korean Human right", *Critical Asian Studies* 46, no.1, (2014): 113-126, DOI: 10.1080/14672715.2014.863580

[5] Kondoch, *The responsibility to Protect and Northeast Asia*, 439.

there, many suffer enslavement, torture, rape, sexual violence, persecution, and other inhumane acts."[6] The correctional facilities and prison camps in the DPRK are organised in a gulag system[7] called kwan-li-so, which counts six structures all over the country and nearly 200.000 prisoners. An outstanding element that I'd like to underline here is the transmission of guilt; indeed, prisoners incarcerated in the labour camps and correctional facilities of the DPRK, transmit their guilt, for the crime they've been found guilty of, to their families that are found guilty by association. At the same time some prisoners are even born in the prison camps and live all their lives in captivity. [8]

Adding to it, the majority of the acts for which North Korean people are punished and incarcerated are not considered crimes in other legal systems of the world, including letting a portrayal of the Great Leader collect dust and crossing the border. Regarding North Koreans leaving the countries without permission, those who are caught by the North Korean or even the Chinese officers are force to repatriate and face severe punishment ranging from imprisonment and torture to execution.[9]

Nevertheless, North Korea has rejected all allegations of human right violations and has highlighted how the government is placing the human person at the centre of its attitude towards human rights and is actively pursuing their realisation[10].

III. North Korea's capability of change

a. The utility of engagement
To understand the meaning of change, as intended in this article, it is useful to think about the interpretations of engagement and coercion of the US and the International Community towards North Korea's nuclear power and then adapt this conception to the question of human rights.

---

[6] Kang, *A Case for the Prosecution of Kim Jong Il for Crimes against Humanity, Genocide, and War Crimes*, 51.
[7] Gulag System inspired to the Soviet labour camps and prisons that housed the political prisoners and criminals of the country
[8] Kondoch, *The responsibility to Protect and Northeast Asia*, 439.
[9] Cha, *The Impossible state*, 170.
[10] Democratic People's Republic of Korea, *National Reports*.

The discourse on the utility of engagement in the North Korean scenario is being debated constantly. Those who think that North Korea is incapable of change, also think that the country will only respond to coercion. The problem is that, even if the International Community has decided to adopt this approach of imposing sanctions on the DPRK, such sanctions have not produced the desired results. As long as the regime maintains its political configuration, it will pose an existential threat to the International Community (IC).[11] Conversely, those who advocate the latter form of engagement and dialogue tend to believe that, with the right set of incentives, is capable of change and in the long period reach a point where it does not represent an existential threat to the IC.

b.   *Conceptions of change and human rights*

The conceptions of change intended as coercion versus dialogue are here applied to the human rights situation in North Korea and can be conceptualised along a continuum. On one hand of this continuum, there are the policymakers who believe that an improvement in the human rights situation in the North Korean context could be perpetrated with a top-down approach. In this kind of approach, it is believed that the recommendations, coming from the International Community and in particular from the Commission of Inquiry, seek to put pressure on the DPRK's government and to promote a change in the country's attitude towards human rights, endorsing an engagement at the UN level. This aforementioned process could lead to the most peaceful sort of change and could represent the most responsible path towards an improvement of the human rights situation within the DPRK.[12]

On the other end of the continuum, there are the majority of North Korean defectors who, deeply understanding the importance of the human rights situation, seek a more direct bottom-up approach[13] oriented towards the creation of a grass root dissident community inside the country. [14]

---

[11] Chubb and Yeo, *Human Rights, nuclear security and the question of engagement in North Korea,* 230

[12] Ibid.

[13] This direct bottom-up approach may also include a coup d'etat and the killing of the North Korean leadership; but this is not analysed in this article as the use of force is not seen as a legitimate human rights strategy.

[14] Cha and Kang, *Nuclear North Korea.*

c.   Bottom-up approach and the role of the International Community

In this article, rather than treating top-down and bottom-up approaches as mutually exclusive, we argue that both approaches are important and we adopt a multidimensional approach based on the consequentiality of the phenomenon.

In the case of the bottom-up strategies, external stakeholders should adopt a more direct approach that, as stated by non-state actors, seeks to bypass the North Korean regime's information blockade and reach the people on the ground. The smuggling of information via DVDs, as well as the distribution of contraband goods and the broadcast of foreign information through short-wave radios, are the basis of this hands-on approach, creating a group of dissidents inside the country, which seeks to undermine the regime and its human rights abuses. [15]

As stated by Yeo and Chubb in their analysis on adaptive activism and transnational advocacy, when the group of dissidents inside the DPRK is finally created, the regime will hypothetically be more open to undertaking a conversation with the International Community within the UN human rights infrastructure; to improve its human rights standards and its local norms and understanding, making them resonate with international law. Indeed, as declared by Yeo and Chubb, if the bottom-up tactics start to take effect, the pressure for greater transparency and greater engagement at the UN level may also start to come from within and not only from the outside.[16] As investigated by Cohen, it's probable that in the long term North Korea's regime will respond to this major pressure coming from within and start to enhance the discourse on human rights with external stakeholders. In a situation where the regime starts to implement serious human rights reforms, it may be necessary for activists to reassess the long-term utility of the subversive tactics.[17]

IV.   From Human Rights to Denuclearization

Numerous studies have focused on the violations perpetrated by the authoritarian government and the sanctions imposed on

---

[15] Chubb and Yeo, *Human Rights, nuclear security and the question of engagement in North Korea,* 232

[16] Chubb and Yeo, *Adaptive Activism.*

[17] Cohen, *Human Rights and Humanitarian Planning.*

the country by the international community; but in doing so, only a few of them have taken into consideration the nuclear issue. Instead, this paper offers a reflection on the question of whether it is possible to pursue human rights objectives at a time of nuclear security contestation. According to it, an improvement of the human rights situation is considered here as a precondition to every possible dialogue over the nuclear threat. Following this rhetoric, we deem that a bottom-up approach aimed at creating a dissident community inside the country should be the first step in dealing with North Korea's human rights situation. Consequently, when a turning point is reached and the regime has been put under internal pressure, the International Community may intervene and collaborate with North Korean officials within the UN human rights infrastructure, thereby bringing minor but steady changes to the country's legal code. [18]

According to Chubb and Yeo, the role of the International Community, which should be developed following actions by internal actors, is essential in implementing a process of mutual trust-building between the IC and the regime, that, in the long period, may also introduce a reduction of US-ROK military joint exercise, thereby leading to a process of lifting sanctions. [19] Gradually, as stated by Milani, this process of trust-building and lifting sanctions will lead to a phase of a more distended dialogue between the IC and the regime and, only at this time, it will be possible to establish a proactive and fruitful discussion regarding denuclearization. [20]
Thus, it is not necessarily true that denuclearization is the direct consequence of solving the human rights situation; but rather an improvement of the North Korean Human rights situation must be a precondition to any denuclearization talk. Even if a denuclearization dialogue is reached, there is no guarantee that a common understanding will be met; due to the different interpretations of denuclearization[21].

---

[18] Chubb and Yeo, *Human Rights, nuclear security and the question of engagement in North Korea,* 232
[19] Ibid.
[20] Milani, *The Evolution of North Korean nuclear program,* 6.
[21]Denuclearization: for the DPRK is the complete denuclearization of the peninsula; for the United States is the denuclearization of the DPRK.

V. **Conclusions**

In this article I have offered a reflection on the question of whether it is possible to pursue human rights objectives at a time of nuclear security contestation. Various non-state networks have to work actively to undermine the regime while creating a dissident community inside the country. If these bottom-up tactics start to take effect, the pressure for greater transparency and engagement at the UN level may start to come from within, rather than solely from outside. At this point in time, the International community may adopt a legal/institutional approach to nudge the regime towards compliance with international human rights standards and in the long term this may lead to an openness of the regime towards denuclearization dialogues.

Bibliography

Amnesty International, North Korea: Political Prison Camps, AI Index, ASA 24/001/2011.

Cha, Victor. *The Impossible State. North Korea Past and Future*. New York: Ecco, 2012.

Cha, Victor, and David Kang. *Nuclear North Korea: A debate on engagement strategies*. Columbia University Press, 2018.

Cohen, Roberta. 2015. "Human Rights and Humanitarian Planning for Crisis in North Korea." *International Journal of Korean Studies* 29 (2): 1–25.

Chubb, Danielle, and Andrew Yeo. "Human rights, nuclear security and the question of engagement with North Korea." *Australian Journal of International Affairs* 73, no. 3 (2019): 227-233.

Chubb, Danielle, and Andrew Yeo. "Adaptive activism: Transnational advocacy networks and the case of North Korea." *North Korean human rights: Activists and networks* (2018): 1-28.

Democratic People's Republic of Korea, National Reports Submitted in Accordance with Paragraph 15 (A) of the Annex to Human Rights Council Resolution 5/1, UN Doc. A/HRC/WG.6/6/PRK/1 of August 27, 2009

Freedom House. "Freedom in the World 2012: The Arab Uprisings and their Global Repercussions",May 8, 2012. http://www.freedomhouse.org/sites/default/files/inline_images / FIW%202012%20Booklet--Final.pdf.

Goedde, Patricia. 2017. "Human Rights Diffusion in North Korea: The Impact of Transnational Legal Mobilization." Asian Journal of Law and Society 5 (1): 1–29.

Human Rights Watch. 2018. "North Korea: Events of 2017", World Report 2018. https://www.hrw. org/world-report/2018/country-chapters/north-korea.

Human Rights Council, The Situation of Human Rights in the Democratic People's Republic of Korea, UN doc. A/HRC/RES/19/13 of April 3, 2012.

Hong, Christine. "War by Other Means: The Violence of North Korean Human Rights." *Asia-Pacific Journal* 12, no. 13 (2014): 1-30.

Kang, Grace. "A Case for the Prosecution of Kim Jong Il for Crimes against Humanity, Genocide, and War Crimes," *Columbia Human Rights Law Review* 38, (2006): 51–80.

Kondoch, Boris. "The responsibility to protect and Northeast Asia: the case of North Korea." In *Post-Conflict Development in East Asia*, pp. 33-50. Routledge, 2016.

Liem, Paul. "Peace as a North Korean Human right", *Critical Asian Studies* 46, no.1, (2014): 113-126, DOI: 10.1080/14672715.2014.863580

Marcus, David. "Famine Crimes in International Law," *AJIL* 97 (2003): 245

Milani, Marco. "The evolution of North Korean Nuclear Program: From survival strategy to ideological legitimization", *ACADEMIC PAPER SERIES* (2018).

UN Human Rights Council. 2014. "Report of the Detailed Findings of the Commission of Inquiry on Human Rights in the Democratic People's Republic of Korea" (2014) A/HRC/25/CRP.1.

US State Department. 2017. Fact Sheet: Prisons of North Korea, Bureau of Democracy, Human Rights and Labor. August 25. https://www.state.gov/j/drl/rls/fs/2017/273647.htm

Yeo, Andrew, and Danielle Chubb, eds. 2018. North Korean Human Rights: Activists and Networks. Cambridge: Cambridge University Press.

Zadeh-Cummings, Nazanin. 2018. "Humanitarians in the Hermit Kingdom: NGOs, Aid, and Access in the DPRK." Unpublished PhD Thesis, City University of Hong Kong.

*****Giulia Rossi***, an MA student of International and Diplomatic Affairs at the University of Bologna-Alma Mater Studiorum, has participated in a simulation of the UN in Rome, in a simulation of the European Parliament in Brussels, and in various meetings with members of the European Parliament such as Marquez and with the Italian Ambassador to the European Union, Benassi. In Spring 2023 she delivered a lectio magistralis at Saint Antony's College, Oxford, on the rise of European populism and the Chinese influence. In March 2023 she participated in the Winter School of the University of Bologna in "Media and Politics in Asia, US and Europe". She has just been accepted to present to the 6th International interdisciplinary conference on "Human Rights, Violence and Dictatorship" organized by Professors of the Gdanzt University and the Sao Paulo University.*

www.ingramcontent.com/pod-product-compliance
Lightning Source LLC
Chambersburg PA
CBHW070951260726
48661CB00003B/1230